ᵒBless Your Stress

It Means You're Still Alive!

For Susan —

*Many blessings
to you!*

More Praise For *Bless Your Stress*

Warning: This book is only masquerading as self-help. Underneath the funny costume is a profound new perspective that can, if you're willing to give up suffering, vastly improve your daily reality. I don't know what they're planning to charge for this book, but it's worth it!
—Mariah Burton Nelson, author of *We Are All Athletes*

Does the world need another book on stress? In a word, yes! This book is light-hearted, thought provoking, and action inviting, all at the same time, making it "jest" perfect for this serious subject. Leslie Charles and Mimi Donaldson have compiled a rich resource of off-beat yet on-target strategies that will help you reflect, relax, rejoice, refresh, rebalance, rekindle, and revitalize your resilience.
—Dr. Joel Goodman, Director, *The Humor Project, Inc.*

Bless Your Stress provides new insights into handling our hectic lives, but most importantly, this book provides readers with easy-to-implement, practical options and healthy choices. A must read for those of us who never give up on achieving a life of balance.
—Betsy Myers, Executive Director, *Center for Public Leadership*
John F. Kennedy School of Government, Harvard University

Bless Your Stress is the bible for stress management. It's the most creative, helpful book on managing stress I've seen—and I've read and taught from all of them for the past 15 years! This book is not just practical and doable; it's fun, funny, and insightful. Bless yourself and buy this book.
—Mary Marcdante, author of *My Mother, My Friend*
and *Living With Enthusiasm*

Bless Your Stress is a blessing in itself, with a truly unique combination of practical strategies and humor for lightening our hearts and lives. You will want to bless your family, friends, and coworkers with the gift of this thoroughly enjoyable book.
—Lori Leyden, Ph.D., M.B.A., author of *The Stress Management*
Handbook: Strategies for Health and Inner Peace

If you're rushing from the minute you wake up to the moment you go to bed…you'll love this witty, fascinating book. *Bless Your Stress* is packed with unique, doable suggestions you can use immediately to create the qulity of life you want now, not someday. Read it and reap.
—Sam Horn, author of *Tongue Fu!*

Any two writers crazy enough to "bless" stress are just brilliant enough to write a book that is chock-a-block filled with advice ranging from the offbeat to the outrageous, and from the powerful to the profound. You'll love the blend of substance and silliness, lightness and depth.
—Eileen McDargh, author of
Work for a Living & Still Be Free to Live and *The Resilient Spirit*

In *Bless Your Stress*, Leslie Charles and Mimi Donaldson explore the primal malady of our time—the experience and feeling of unrelenting stress—offering pithy observations, profound insights, and entirely practical solutions.
—Jeff Davidson, M.B.A., C.M.C., author of
The Joy of Simple Living and *The 60 Second Procrastinator*

Thanks to reading *Bless Your Stress*, my to-do list just got shorter. This book will make a perfect gift for all of my multi-tasking, time juggling friends—maybe they will get the message loud and clear, just as I did. I especially liked the practical, usable tips and wonderful humor.
—Patty DeDominic, past President
National Association of Women Business Owners

Your ability to turn stress into energy and vitality determines the quality of your life. This wonderful book shows you how to take complete charge of your mind, emotions, and relationships.
—Brian Tracy, author of *The Power of Charm*

Life is full of bumpy roads, but this delightful guidebook written by two smart, witty tour guides will not only keep you on course—you'll smile and laugh your way through the journey. Five stars!
—Chellie Campbell, author of *The Wealthy Spirit*
and *Zero to Zillionaire*

Bless Your Stress is a fun, well-written romp that outpaces other books in its field. Who would have thought that handling stress could be approached in such a clever, imaginative, or enjoyable manner? This book makes a terrific gift for the cranky, stressed out people in your life!
—Judy Carter, author of *The Comedy Bible*

*O*A Special Word from the Authors

O If the only joy in your life is found in a bottle of dish washing liquid, don't despair. If feeling pressed and duressed has become a daily routine and your stress level can leap tall buildings in a single bound, don't worry. There's still hope. This unusual and enjoyable book will transport you to a kinder, gentler world where you can live, love, and work in a more resilient and revitalized state.

O Sound good? It is. Sound impossible? It isn't. This is a fun read, designed to entertain and enlighten you, but be warned—if you have a bad case of the gloomies and don't want to have a good time, *Bless Your Stress* is not for you.

O But wait. There's a reason you picked up this book. What deep subconscious need guided your eyes or hand toward this title? If you're looking for simple, straightforward solutions to help lighten your stress load, *Bless Your Stress* has them.

O You'll discover ways to ease the conflicts you face every day. You'll be better able to curb your racing mind or rapid heartbeat and stop that sense of being out of synch and never catching up. You'll regain some control over your life and have a great time along the way. It's almost as simple as pushing a button.

O If you have more stress than you want, but still manage to maintain a good sense of humor in spite of it all; if you appreciate playful, practical ideas, then walk, don't run— we don't want you to hurt yourself—to the bookstore counter, buy this book, take it home, and start reading. You'll be glad you did, and so will everyone else in your life.

ALSO BY C. LESLIE CHARLES

All Is Not Lost
Why Is Everyone So Cranky?
The Instant Trainer
Rule # One
The Customer Service Companion
The Customer Service Companion Study Guide
Stick To It!

ALSO BY Mimi Donaldon

Negotiating For Dummies

Bless Your Stress

It Means You're Still Alive!

C. Leslie Charles

Mimi Donaldson

Yes! Press
East Lansing, MI

Bless Your Stress

Published by:

Yes! Press

P.O. Box 956
East Lansing, MI 48826
517.675.7535
www.BlessYourStress.com

Cartoons by Leigh Rubin
Cover Design by Diana L. Grinwis
Cover Portrait of Leslie Charles by J.D. Small
Cover Portrait of Mimi Donaldson by Debra Gerson

Printed and bound by
McNaughton & Gunn, Inc., Saline MI

Publisher's Cataloging in Publication Data

Charles, C. Leslie.
  Bless your stress : it means you're still alive! / C.
Leslie Charles & Mimi Donaldson. -- 1st ed.
    p. cm.
  ISBN 13   978-0-9644621-4-4
  ISBN 10   0-9644621-4-1

  1. Stress (Psychology) 2. Stress management
I. Donaldson, Mimi. II. Title

BF575.S75C438 2006   158.1
                          QBI06-600053

Library of Congress Catalog Card Number on file

First Edition
10 9 8 7 6 5 4 3 2 1

From Mimi...

To my nieces and nephews: Adam, Tanya, Hayley, Matthew, Emma and Mark (the REAL writer of the family). All of you, in your own way, have taught me many lessons about blessing—and stressing.

From Leslie...

To my parents: I gave you many opportunities to bless your stress while growing up. And to my kids, who in turn, gave me many opportunities to bless mine.

About the Author

Leslie Charles, award-winning professional speaker, has educated and entertained audiences throughout North America for over three decades. Because Leslie thinks learning should be enjoyable and invigorating, her customized keynotes and workshops both delight and enlighten audiences. Not only is Leslie a skilled speaker, she's an accomplished writer. *Bless Your Stress* is her eighth book.

Following the release of her critically acclaimed *Why Is Everyone So Cranky?*, Leslie enjoyed extensive media attention, with national TV appearances, radio shows, numerous magazines and newspapers, and a USA Today cover story.

Once a teen bride and mother, two-time high school dropout, displaced homemaker, and welfare recipient, Leslie has faced the stress bully and prevailed. Her book, *All Is Not Lost*, is dedicated to her son, Robbie, killed in a work accident in 1984. Leslie speaks and writes with gentle authority on maintaining a resourceful and resilient spirit, in spite of it all. She is a contributing author to *Chicken Soup for the Single Parent's Soul*.

A lifelong Lansing, Michigan area resident, Leslie enjoys horseback riding, reading, disc golf, and enjoying nature in her four-acre mini wildlife preserve. Her newest pursuit is designing and creating inspirational bracelets. Leslie ingeniously combines this talent with her writing skills: every bracelet comes with an original story or poem, connecting meaning and purpose to the design. Yes, there is a "Bless Your Stress" bracelet!

To contact Leslie about a presentation for your organization, to read samplings of her other books, to review her inspirational bracelets, or to simply say hello, please visit:

www.LeslieCharles.com
www.PreciousPurpose.com
www.BlessYourStress.com
www.WhyIsEveryoneSoCranky.com
leschas@aol.com.
517.675.7535

About the Author

Mimi Donaldson was raised with a comedic view of the world, thanks to early exposure to the fabulous comedy of Sid Caesar, Imogene Coca, Milton Berle, and Lenny Bruce. As children, Mimi and her brother performed comedy sketches around the house.

Mom and dad thought their daughter was destined for greatness. "One day you'll be a star," her mother would tell her, not knowing Mimi would one day entertain people in suits all day long. Mimi's father, a physician, once told her, "What you do is a mixture of mental health and show biz." He was right.

Mimi excites, educates and entertains audiences around the world, sharing the stage with the likes of Colin Powell, Elizabeth Dole, and Maya Angelou. She has thrilled and inspired over half of the Fortune 500 companies.

Before starting her consulting business in 1984, she spent 10 years as a Human Resources Trainer at Northrop Aircraft, Rockwell International, and Walt Disney Productions. Mimi has a B.A. in Speech and Communications from the University of Iowa and a Masters Degree in Education from Columbia University. Mimi is coauthor of the best selling *Negotiating for Dummies,* and was recently a visiting professor at Harvard University's Center for Public Leadership at the Kennedy School of Government.

Mimi has been blessing her stress for the last six years. It's helped her stay upbeat and positive through divorce, illness, hospitalization, parental health issues, 9/11, employee debacles, a crashed hard drive, and other adventures.

When not speaking, Mimi enjoys traveling to exotic locales and collecting Asian art, in particular ningyo, Japanese figurines.

To talk with Mimi about a presentation for your organization, or to learn more about Mimi and her products, please contact her at:
www.MimiDonaldson.com
mimi@mimidonaldson.com.
310.577.0229

Acknowledgments

It takes a village to raise a book and there are many people to thank for their assistance in making *Bless Your Stress* all that it is. Special thanks to Rob Carr, our man in publishing, for editing and transforming our manuscript into a book.

From Leslie's neighborhood, thank you, Carol Mase, for adding finesse, and Mary Bradshaw for your little touches. Hugs to my stress-prone granddaughter, Ashley Kuripla, who read the manuscript in its infancy.

Thanks for your stories and remarks: Sharon Adcock, Mike McKinley, Ann (you know who you are), Sally Peters, Dolores Hayden, Brenda Betts, Everett Zack, Susan Prorak, Stephen Tweed, and Elizabeth Jeffries. Thank you for your inspiration, Susan RoAne, Mary Marcdante, Sam Horn, Marilynn Semonick, Mariah Burton Nelson, and my mom, Julie.

Thanks to Tara Nofziger, my wonderful miracle-working web maestra, who helped me launch www.BlessYourStress.com while preparing for her unexpected business trip to Asia.

From Mimi's side of the street, a huge thank you goes to Lisa Becker, or as Leslie and I think of her, "LTM" (Lisa the Magnificent), for your early research, and especially for finding the impossible.

Thank you to my parents whose existence on this planet I bless every day.

Thank you for your contributions—and laughs: Sarina Simon, Judy Carter, Pat Neubacher, Lynne Romanowski, Lori Leyden, Elizabeth Davidson, Dana Ehrlich, Susan Sloane, and Larry Richard.

And from both of us, everlasting mega-kudos to Debbie Riley for your magical, masterful editing. Your English teachers and professors would be proud of you! From now on, whenever we commit word to paper, we shall each be asking ourselves, WWDD (what would Debbie do?).

$\mathcal{O}$Contents

A Special Word from the Authors
$\mathcal{O}$ A friendly dose of stress relief: just what you've been looking for

Introduction
$\mathcal{O}$ A look at the curious ways we human beings deal with stress
$\mathcal{O}$ The good news about stress and why you want it in your life

Introduction

The obscure we see eventually.
The completely obvious takes longer.
—Edwin Newman

How many people do you know who are consistently relaxed, healthy, having fun, and fully enjoying life? Do you even know anyone who fits this description? But here's the real question: if you compiled such a list, would your name be on the roster? If so, you'll love this book for what it has to say. If not, you *need* this book for what it has to say!

Despite the serious nature of this topic, we promise that *Bless Your Stress* will make you nod in agreement, smile in amusement, and maybe laugh out loud. It will also inspire you into action. This book will help you discover how you unknowingly create and maybe even perpetuate your stress. It will help you break the stress cycle and create a more fulfilling future.

If you can relate to any of the following, this book is for you:

O *You finally find time for a ten-minute break to breathe and relax like the stress experts suggest but after three minutes you're more stressed than before you sat down. This is because you can't stop thinking about everything you should be getting done right now instead of sitting there like a lump, doing nothing.*

O *You spend more time than you care to admit thinking how great life would be if your boss, neighbor, coworker, or a certain family member were to undergo a massive personality transplant.*

O   You finally start your new diet on Monday, but by Friday you blow it so badly that you compulsively stuff yourself all weekend. You end up feeling fatter and more desperate than you were the week before.

Sound familiar? See, we said you're not alone. We all have our contradictory ways of trying to handle our pressure cooker lives, and some of them don't work terribly well. Got stress? If so, you're in good company.

These days, stress is more common than the common cold and more plentiful than political pundits in an election year. So stick around: you'll discover the good news (and the bad news) about stress, how it fits in your life, and how you can whittle it down to size. You'll be glad you did.

Of course, you already know that every day can't be picture perfect. Just like chocolate cake, sex, and Super Bowls, some are better than others. But relief is in sight, and it doesn't come in a capsule or bottle; it comes from you. Just read this book a bit at a time, try these ideas, and we guarantee things will improve, even on the days when stress chooses to raise its prickly little head.

Maybe you've read other books on stress but some of them actually made you feel worse, not better, because they listed all the horrendous things that could happen to you if you didn't calm down. Instead of relaxing, you began worrying about the grim health complications you hadn't even known about until now.

So much for "knowledge is power"! Well, this book won't scare or threaten you. It will inform and encourage you with easy, enjoyable methods to relieve the pressure and bring your life back into balance. There's an old saying that you can't add more days to your life, but you can certainly add more life to your days.

Yes, stress is serious business, and we have a lot of legitimate reasons to feel uneasy, especially since September 11, 2001. But a quick historical rewind reveals that we were pretty stressed out before then.

Recall the nineties: the economy was buzzing along, the Cold War was long since over, jobs were plentiful, and our soil had not yet been terrorized. Yet, the word *rage* was constantly in the headlines and public outbursts were everywhere, not just on those in-your-face talk shows. It was as if the less we had to worry about, the more we found to complain about.

Ironically, some things have improved since then. For the most part, road rage has been racheted down to plain rudeness, possibly because drivers are so busy blathering on their cell phones they no longer notice the things that used to make them mad. And then there's reality TV, where viewers can worry about the truly significant social questions of our time, such as who goes and who stays, who's hot, and who's not, who sizzles and who fizzles.

But gee, isn't there more to life than witnessing other people's desperate attempts to hit the winner's circle in the celebrity lotto? Aren't there bigger things to care about, like world hunger, pandemic disease, or finding a pair of pants that makes you look ten pounds thinner? Despite today's serious issues, perhaps because of them, we're better off not taking every minute of every day too seriously.

Author Norman Cousins proved that laughter is the best medicine. He brought himself back from a near-death condition by entertaining himself with an ongoing film festival of classic comedies that kept him in a state of merriment. Thanks to his grit and creativity, not only did Cousins recover from a life-threating illness, he extended his life and became an expert on the mind's capacity for healing. His phenomenal book, *Head First*, chronicles what he learned about the power of the mind-body connection during his years at UCLA.

Social wits and humorists such as Mark Twain, Will Rogers, Mae West, Lily Tomlin, and George Carlin built their careers by emphasizing the humor of human existence, even when it hurts. Julia Sweeney's funny and disarming one-woman show, *God Said Ha!*, is about cancer and death. *Only the Truth is Funny*, by comedian Rick Roberts, is stark, thought provoking, and hysterical.

Pain and laughter are tightly interwoven into the fabric of life, and if stress is as old as humankind, humor must be, too. In fact, your ability to laugh is essential for reducing stress. Maybe instead of shooting for a long lifetime, you should hope for a long "laughtime" instead.

We have always possessed both the ability (and the need) to laugh. It's no accident that there's a Comedy Channel and local comedy clubs where we can go forget our troubles for a few hours. The more stressful and serious a society becomes, the greater the need for relief.

Are we suggesting that you should eliminate all of the tension in your life? No, and you wouldn't want to. You see, death is nature's way of telling you to slow down. The *only* completely and totally stress-free zone that exists is a cemetery (for the residents, that is). In other words, absolutely *no* stress means you're now riding the Pale Horse, hitchhiking with the Grim Reaper, cooling down with the Big Chill. Do these bleak images make you feel at least a wee bit better about the stress in your life? We hope so!

Hey, if you're still able to gaze down at the green grass instead of staring up at its brown underbelly, this in itself is something to celebrate. After all, a bad day alive beats the heck out of a good day dead! So we're not going for *utterly* stress-free here, just a lower ratio. Like the story of the three bears, you don't want your stress load too big (overwhelm) or too small (boredom). You want it to be just right. Maybe it would help if you thought of stress as life's way of giving you a friendly nod. *Howdy partner! Grab a chair and sit a spell. Relax. Put your feet up and take a load off.*

While stress comes wrapped in a bonus package of physical side effects, we won't focus on that. We're not doctors and we don't intend to scare you into bouts of insomnia or panic attacks by citing scary statistics or symptoms. The last thing we want is to find you huddled in a corner inhaling a plate of mashed potatoes or a package of Oreos to ease your anxiety.

"Stress eating?" you say, "How did they know?" Easy. While most naturally thin people lose their appetites when stressed (bless their skinny little hearts), not even the most well-adjusted individuals go on broccoli binges or meditation marathons when their stress level is off the charts. If only!

It's way more typical to head for the comfort foods,

wolfing down exactly what we don't need: the gooey, the chewy, the crunchy, the munchy, the salty, the faulty. When the chips are down, reach for the chips! Yup, it makes no sense, and why should it? You could call this contrariness the curse of free will, but few of us have perfect impulse control. Human nature being what it is, you may often find yourself doing the complete opposite of what's ideal. Welcome to the club.

We all know that life is a mixed blessing. Joy and sorrow. Good and bad. Up and down. Blessed and stressed. But some people don't recognize when they're in the middle of the blessed times. It's easy to obsess over things that don't really count: a drippy faucet, lousy drivers, slow lines, bad hair days, ruined manicures, traffic jams, spinach between your teeth, or weather warnings interrupting your favorite TV show.

When you focus on the little things that are wrong instead of the big things that are right in your life, it's easy to get jaded and off center. That's why we wrote *Bless Your Stress*. It's a great place to visit for a mental tune up or attitude adjustment, a little like happy hour without the booze. We hope you'll belly up to this book, stick around awhile, and enjoy this wise and witty blend of novel ideas designed to bring you lasting relief.

Bless Your Stress

It Means You're Still Alive!

Chapter 1
Too Stressed to be Blessed?

RUBES ™   By Leigh Rubin

Creators Syndicate, Inc.
© 1997 Leigh Rubin!

cre8ors@aol.com

"What a lousy trip ... it rained the *whole* time!"

Chapter 1
Too Stressed to be Blessed?

If you can't be a good example,
then you'll just have to be a terrible warning.
—Catherine Aird

Distress Calls

If there's one word that describes our society, it is stress. Hurried, harried, and too busy, many of our citizens find themselves in a persistent state of overwhelm, overload, and distraction. Like lapsing into a momentary ADD-like state, they get busy, they get preoccupied, they don't pay attention, they make mistakes, they blame themselves for their mistakes (or somebody else does), their stress goes up, and so it goes. This doesn't sound familiar, does it?

It's true for all of us. There are times when stress seems to materialize out of nowhere and take over, like some shape-shifting alien who entraps you in its force field. During these episodes, you may feel helplessly caught up in the hustle and bustle of the moment, unable to rescue yourself from its clutches.

Here are three true-to-life stress stories—maybe you can relate.

A couple heading for their first dog show backs out of the driveway, their van packed to the gills with dog food, cages, grooming supplies—everything but their sofa. Suddenly they see the face of their left-behind show puppy, nose pressed to the living room window, tail slowly wagging, a forlorn look on its face.

A man sits in the car, waiting to pick up his wife after work, when a complete stranger jumps in and then screams when she realizes this isn't her car and he isn't her husband.

A woman pulls into the drive-thru lane, orders her McMorning meal, stops at the first window, exchanges pleasantries, pays for her food, and then blithely drives away. Two miles later, she realizes she cruised right past the second window, abandoning the order she so happily paid for.

Even our friend, Sharon Adcock, an international consultant and usually responsible adult, admits she, too, isn't exempt from such absent-minded moments. Returning home from an early morning business flight, she paid the taxi driver, jumped out of the cab, hurried into her apartment through the garage, and discovered that her car was missing.

No, it hadn't been stolen—her vehicle was still cooling its wheels in the LAX parking lot, right where she had left it. Still under the influence from two weeks of overnight business trips where taxis had carted her back and forth, Sharon had completely forgotten about driving to the airport that very morning.

Before you start tsking or wondering how people could be so dense, let's go on with our list of stressed out human tricks. Maybe you've wasted ten minutes of precious time looking for your eyeglasses when they were actually on your head, or you tried to put a pair of specs over the ones you were wearing.

Perhaps you have panicked when, during a family outing, you realized your toddler was nowhere in sight, until your spouse confided that the kid was on your back. Or it could be that more than once, you've tried to open the door to your house by clicking your car remote. Need we go on?

No need for banner headlines on any of the incidents described here; they all indicate symptoms of stress over-load. Go ahead and laugh, and then review the last four months of your own life. Heave a sigh of relief that we haven't been watching you!

A Lot of Nerve

Though stress has always been a part of the curious condition called life, it wasn't always so commonplace, nor so extreme. There was a time, not so long ago, when people would make a vague statement such as, "My nerves have been bothering me lately," and that was pretty much the end of it. No rants. No fussing. No trips to the medicine cabinet. No calls to the family physician begging for a pre-scription. No one claiming that they were in even worse shape. This was the way life was and you just accepted it: sometimes your nerves bothered you and most of the time they didn't.

Well, you can't get away with a simple little statement like that today. Once the word "stress" became a part of our vocabulary, things began to change. It worked its way up the corporate ladder and got a promotion. It became real. After all, stress sounds far more serious than a little case of nerves. It's now an official condition with an extensive as-sortment of pharmaceuticals for treating it. Stress is now something we worry about, talk about, obsess about. And we've gotten really good at it.

The Stress Olympics: I Coulda Been a Contender

Today, bring up the subject of stress and people perk

up. Like victims of Stockholm Syndrome, some confused souls get unnaturally attached to their stress. If you could read their thoughts you'd hear something like, "They're talking about *me!* I'm stressed! Let me play!" Ready for action, they can't wait to jump off the bench and into the stress relay lane with a "You think you've got it bad!" or "Let me tell you what a rotten week I had!" Then follows the competition over who's the most stressed. Does this sound farfetched? Just mention the word next time you're out to dinner or at a party. Then grab your stopwatch, get out of the way, and let the games begin.

Here's another form of cheap entertainment: during a casual conversation, mention how busy you are and wait for the reactions. "Oh, that's nothing! Last week, I..." or "Hey, my life's so hectic I haven't had a good night's sleep since the first Bush administration!" At work, you might witness two coworkers, Blackberries or PDAs in hand, going to the mat over who is the busiest and most overloaded. The problem with this kind of competition is that no one ends up truly happy about winning this losing game. Nay, we say. There are better choices!

If you find yourself an unwitting player in the Stress Olympics, disqualify yourself. Think of this audacious move as taking off the track shoes and putting on your fuzzy slippers. Now that you're no longer in the race, maybe you'll appreciate these suggestions:

O   *Every day, spend a few minutes decompressing instead of obsessing over how busy or stressed you are.*

O   *Don't let others taunt you into competitive comparisons of stress burdens or busyness.*

𝒪   *Focus on what's right in your life instead of keeping track of the frustrations or irritations.*

𝒪   *Give yourself permission to learn that saying no to others is a way of saying yes to yourself.*

𝒪   *Block out sections of your calendar for "self" time and stick to it.*

𝒪   *When asked to compromise that time, say you have a commitment. No one needs to know it's just for you.*

𝒪   *Bless yourself whenever you ease out of the fast lane, even if it's only for a lap or two.*

Hey, it's a small start, but you know that the little things in life can make a big difference down the road. Let the new game begin!

Break the Rut: Go Slow Mo

While we're doling out some early tips, try this on for size: quit being in a hurry wherever you go. In the South they say, "Walk slow and stay in the shade." This is good advice, and it works. Teach yourself to hurry slowly. It's more efficient and effective than rushing, mushing, and hurling yourself toward your destination as if you were a heat-seeking missile. Breathe, relax, and smile more. Take your foot off the gas. Look around. You'll find less traffic, less hassle, less stress.

People often stay in the same rut, even if what they're doing isn't working all that well. A friend of ours commented during her annual exam that her hip had been bothering her. When her doctor asked, "What have you been doing for it?" she replied, "Complaining!"

Well, perhaps you've heard the definition of insanity as doing the same thing over and over again while expecting (but never getting) different results. We say be outrageous—try something new. Step out of the mold before your habits harden (or you do). You may just astonish yourself and confuse others. Doesn't that sound like fun?

Some Good News About Stress

It's time to offer our definition of this thing called stress, just so we're all on the same page. Stress is and always has been a part of life. It's natural, organic, hard-wired, and older than George Hamilton. Every living creature on earth experiences stress (well, maybe not cats). When your heart rate hikes up or you feel a shot of adrenaline, you can take solace in considering these physical reactions as an undeniable and hopeful sign that you are still able to feed and dress yourself.

This is a good thing! You have not yet turned onto that final Off Ramp or been disappeared by the big Delete Button in the sky. Your body has not yet assumed room temperature. You're still vertical. Remember the old saying, "Where there's life, there's hope." Well, yeah! There's a lot of hope here. And while it's true that feeling stressed is not your favorite state, it's not entirely a bad thing. Stress just is, and you want to maintain the level that works best for you.

Borrowing from the work of the stress pioneer, Dr. Hans Selye, stress is a reaction to what's happening around you. Simply put, it is energy. When you feel a stress surge, you're having an energy crisis—an abundance rather than a scarcity. The question is not, "Will you have stress?" but rather, "How much?"

And you have a lot of say in that. Guess what: you can manage those moments when you end up with more energy than you think you deserve. And given that stress is a symptom of the blissful state of being alive, you'll never want to leave home without it.

Hanging by a Thread

Dealing with stress is simply an issue of sensible choice and conscious containment. If you've ever made the bad fashion choice of wearing a pair of pants that were too tight, you know what stress is. You had to suck it in to put them on, or lie down so you could zip them up. You were afraid to take a deep breath, fearing that the seams might explode.

But thanks to a shoddy combination of desperation, haste, and poor judgment, you wore them anyway, painfully aware of even the slightest gesture. Maybe you lucked out and everything held together. But how much fun was it, remaining so tense and vigilant, contracting every muscle and ounce of fat every time you made a drastic move like breathing and standing, or God forbid, sneezing?

This illustrates what happens when too much energy gets stored up in too small a space. Even if things don't give out, there's a good deal of strain, wear, and tear. Like a seam stretched to the max, your brain and body can only handle so much pressure. There's a point where something's got to give. It doesn't have to be this way. Life is too short to spend it being stressed. Unless Shirley MacLaine is right, you only go around once, so why not travel in comfort?

We're not saying that life is perfect. In today's unstable, ever-changing world, you face many genuine concerns: geopolitical issues, job security, relationships, money, personal safety, health problems, and the possibility that Kim Delaney might attempt another TV series. But with the proper outlook and a willingness to take care of yourself, you can handle these pressures and more.

Know Thy Stress

Now that we've defined stress, we need to acknowledge that some people don't fully get what it is and isn't, and how it does or doesn't fit into their lives. Some think the goal is to get rid of all their stress. But considering what that really means (hint: the Deep Sleep from which we never awaken), that's not really what they're looking for.

Some people just figure that life is chock full of stress and that's the way it is. They spend their days in a flurry, multitasking, interrupting themselves and others, working extra hours, relentlessly pushing themselves, clueless about how tightly they are wound.

Others suffer in silence, enduring physical symptoms and chronic mental distress, thinking there's nothing that can be done. For all those needy souls who could use some clarification—and relief—this is the perfect time to dispel some common myths about stress.

Myth-Guided Notions About Stress

1.) Stress is Bad and I Shouldn't Have Any.
Stress is not like Batman, Wonder Woman, Freddie, or the Hulk. It's not a super hero, "shero," or villain. It's not good or bad, it just is. Think of stress as a constant and ongoing sign of life, and if you aren't experiencing at least a little bit now and then, check your pulse to make sure you're still kicking. Have someone else check if you're not sure.

2.) Stress Means Something is Wrong With Me.

To be honest, there could be something wrong with you, perhaps many things actually, but we're only concerned about your level of stress right now. Carefully examine how tense or pressured you feel most of the time so you can gauge if the stress in your life is energizing or exhausting you. If it's the latter, take a deep breath, relax, and read on.

3.) Stress is the Same For Everyone.

Just as we are tall or small, wide or wafer thin, pale-skinned or colorful, bright or dull, rich or broke, famous or unknown, stress is unique to the individual. In facing the same situation, one person may feel blessed, while another feels stressed: "Yum—liver and onions!" versus "Yuk—no way do I eat organ meat!" When it comes to interpreting life's experiences, one size does not fit all; we each have our own way of looking at things.

The nature of the stress also differs. You could say there's "real" stress: being diagnosed with a life-threatening disease, recovering from a serious accident, dealing with a chronic illness, caregiving an ailing parent or child, losing your job. If huge, life-altering circumstances such as these were to happen, chances are you would somehow summon the fortitude to face them one day at a time.

The stress we want to help you shed comes from too much emphasis on life's little annoyances: bad drivers, bad service, bad hair days, bad weather. We call them the "awful inevitables" and sometimes an impulsive reaction on your part can have unintended consequences, creating more stress than the original incident.

You'll also want to shrug off the social stress of too much

wanting, striving, doing, and expecting that is so common in our culture. You could call this the "curse of plenty." The purpose of this book is to help whittle your stress load down to the exact size you look and feel best in, just like your favorite pair of jeans.

4.) Stress is Caused By Things Outside of You.

Stress isn't a mysterious airborne microbe, nor is it a vicious virus you can catch from that cranky person in the cubicle next to you at work. Stress resides in your body, kindly brought to you by your very own mind. Every day you experience a bounty of triggering events that can potentially generate a stress reaction. But always remember—you don't actually "catch" stress, you create it.

While stress can be set off by external forces, you are the one who either engages with, or walks away, from the stressor. You are your very own stress factory, capable of producing or reducing it. You can consciously keep output at appropriate levels or unknowingly step up the operation to a wild, 24/7 full-scale mass production. Think about it: who really needs to walk around with a "Go ahead...make my day," chip on their shoulder the size of Manhattan?

5.) I Can't Do Anything About My Stress So Why Try.

You eat when you're hungry, sleep when you're tired, and drink when you're thirsty, right? This means you've got a handle on how to take care of your basic needs. Add stress to that list and pay more attention to your body's symptoms and signals. Become intimately familiar with how you feel mentally and physically when you're calm and comfy, so you can quickly detect when you're not.

In effect, you become your own stress S.W.A.T. team.

You'll be able to head off your anxiety at the pass so it can't take you hostage. Being able to quickly recognize signs of tension or anxiety is essential for shifting from stressing to blessing.

6.) I Don't Have Time to Bless My Stress.

Funny, you have time to repress your stress (deny or rationalize) and express your stress (rant or gripe) to family and friends, right? So instead, why not take some of that time to decompress your stress (address it, less it, finesse it) so you can blow off some of those unavoidable hassles instead of letting them bug you.

7.) Stress is a Part of Human Suffering.

If you're into brain bondage, then we are pleased to present the new shrinking stress charm bracelet that gets tighter and tighter throughout the day. There's one with crimps for those who don't know how to feel bad enough on their own; operators are standing by.

The truth is, in more cases than most of us realize, misery comes down to choice. Yes, bad things happen. You may suffer loss, disappointment, and other challenges, but you are not obligated to remain in pain. Even shattered hearts can heal. As the saying goes, change is inevitable, misery is optional.

8.) If I Won the Lotto I'd be Free of Stress For Good.

Oh yeah? There are books that tell the stories of lotto winners and how life tanked for many of them after they won the jackpot. As hard as it is to believe, a high percentage of big money winners end up hopelessly in debt and alienated from friends and family, ending up with far more regrets than rewards.

It sounds like a cliché, but money isn't the answer to everything and some of the best things in life are still free. Air, for one. Take a nice deep breath, and lavish yourself in this abundant, essential, cost-free luxury!

9.) Stress Relief Comes In a Package.

If you're looking for short-term relief, pop a pill, or a few even, but if you want results for the long term, look in the mirror. Your most powerful antidote for treating stress is looking back at you, and what a fine-looking blend of special ingredients you are! Preen a moment if you must, strut your best stuff. Show off. Play air guitar, do the moon walk. How do you spell relief? M-E! It's the finest product on the market, no prescription is needed, and the supply will last as long as you do. Even Costco can't give you a better deal than this!

10.) Stress Goes With My Horoscope.

Here's a flash: your stress level is not the result of your sun sign, nor is it connected to your rising sign. You can't blame it all on your gene pool either. Stress is largely your call. Whether your stress level goes up or down (or sideways) connects directly to the unconscious habits, perceptions, and patterns you've built through the years.

Attitude, lifestyle, and health practices are all linked to your level of stress. The good news is that while you can't change your horoscope or genetic makeup, you can change your mind and your habits. Anything you've learned in life, you can unlearn and relearn, and there are untold benefits in choosing to do so.

11.) I Wouldn't be Stressed if I Were Famous.

Fame can cause more stress than it relieves, even the

momentary flashes of fame enjoyed by contestants on reality TV shows. Hey, once their stint is over, it's all downhill from there. But you're still on the "up" side of the grade. There are all kinds of possibilities for you, even if you never make it to the little screen.

Take a hard look sometime at the list of not so well-adjusted celebrities you read about in magazines: the ones who struggle with serial romances, disposable marriages, strings of divorces, alcohol or drug issues, inner demons, personal tragedies, and even suicide. Are you sure you could handle all that bliss?

12.) My Stress Will Go Away on Its Own.

You're right. When you heave your last labored breath, all your stress will disappear. Are you sure you want to wait so long or would you like to take a shot at handling it while you're still able to activate a heart monitor?

13.) They Didn't Have Stress in the Good Old Days.

Wanna bet? People died before they were old enough to talk about it! Remember all those wars you read about in history class? You think there was a little stress for the unlucky lot who faced lions or gladiators in the Coliseum? Does the name Pompeii ring a bell? How about the Black Plague or the Great Depression?

Do you suppose that amputations without anesthesia and the threat of death by childbirth caused a wee bit of anxiety back then? If you lived before the 20th century and were over thirty, you'd be dead by now. Or too feeble to hold this book. Of course, even if you could hold this book you couldn't read it (so much for illiteracy). Is that enough of the good old days for you?

14.) I Can't Wait Any Longer—I Want My Stress to Disappear Right Now, If Not Sooner.

We wish we could make your stress go missing, but alas, that's not possible. If you're hoping for an instant miracle stress cure like you might see advertised in an infomercial or e-mail subject line, forget it. We're sorry, but only morphine works that fast. Truth be told, it took you a while to reach your current state of stress, and it will take a little time to turn your condition around.

Just like exercise equipment, this book won't work by osmosis. In fact, you can't even use it to hang clothes on. *Bless Your Stress* won't do you much good unless you're willing to read it and actually try these ideas.

But you can improve your stress situation, and that's the point. Stay with us. In the meantime, whenever you feel the need, take a nice deep breath and force a little smile. Think about things in your life you feel good about, in spite of your stress. If things are extreme right now and you feel at the end of your rope, tie a knot in it and hold on. You're in for a good ride.

About Blessing Your Stress

At this point you may be wondering what we, your authors, mean when we say "bless your stress." But there's a more important question: what does the word *bless* mean to you? We want to reach and touch as many readers as possible. We want you to personally identify with the ideas in this book. Rather than imposing a single or precise definition of what it means to bless your stress, we invite you to use your own.

Every time you read the word "bless" think of what it

means to you. Embrace it. Internalize it. Bring all your faith, philosophy, and feelings into the picture, so you can make reading this book the most meaningful, transformative experience possible.

Take Note

Now that we've put things in perspective, we encourage you to begin a Bless Your Stress journal so you can record your thoughts while you read this book. If you've never kept a journal, this is a great time to begin.

As you read this book, ideas will pop into your head and if you don't write them down, they'll be forgotten. Journaling your way through a book is a handy method for increasing self-awareness, which is the first step in making any significant change.

Whenever you find yourself becoming anxious or tense, take the time to identify what you're feeling and why. Write about these instances when you have a moment and describe how they affect you: thoughts, feelings, physical indicators. In a few months, you'll be able to look back, review your journal, and gauge your progress.

This is one of the many benefits of journaling. But you don't have to stop there. Personalize this book. Underline passages or phrases that resonate. Highlight the sentences that seem custom written for you. Dog ear the pages. Make notes in the margins, mark it up—we don't mind! In fact, we encourage you to share your favorite parts of this book with others, especially someone you love.

The Good News About Stress

So here it is. Stress is a part of life; it's here to stay. We'd like to think you are, too, for as long as you can, and we'd like to help you to do it in style. Yes, stress is an issue for all of us, but hope and salvation are waiting in the wings. You see, in the past, experts have told us to manage our stress, embrace it, control it, release it, harness it, channel it, and transform it, but until now, *no one has dared to bless it!*

Look up the word "bless" in a good dictionary. Beyond the first definitions, you will find that the words bless and blessing are synonyms for gratitude and happiness. In other words, by blessing your stress you establish the foundation for your own happiness.

Blessing your stress is an affirmation of your existence, acknowledgment of life's mixed bag, an openness to all of life's experiences, and armament for facing up to the tough stuff. Blessing your stress is a way of refusing to let the little, inconsequential irritations corrode the quality of your days. The more you bless, the more you let go of your stress.

From Then to Now

Just as stress is as old as humankind, so is blessing. From the beginning of time, we've possessed the ability to shake it off and start over if we choose, and what a gift this is. Consider how hazardous and stressful life was for people in ancient times, but they didn't waste their breath ranting about it.

Julius Caesar didn't complain about bad haircuts, nor did Joan of Arc worry if her suit of armor made her look fat. People of the past were too busy dealing with the basics of life and death to obsess over trivial things. Today, millions of people on this earth are still living on the edge, enduring conditions so harsh and relentless we can't even imagine.

It's a sobering thought (and a worthwhile one), to realize there are individuals on this planet who don't consider it the end of the world when a family member forgets to pull the hamburger out of the freezer (what hamburger; what freezer?), messes up the remote for the cable TV (what remote; what TV?), or forgets to turn on the air conditioner before leaving the house (what air; what house?).

It's sad that so many people in this plentiful culture of ours behave as if they're living on the brink of extinction when they're so far from real hardship they can't even comprehend it. These individuals are long on expectation and short on gratitude. They don't realize how much better their lives would be if it were the other way around.

Bless the Stressed

Let's take one last swipe at history and the stresses faced by those who pushed the limits. What if Columbus had decided to only play near the shore because he was afraid of getting lost? What if John Wesley Powell or Lewis and Clark had said, "I can't go exploring—I might get hurt or run out of food, and that would be very stressful!" What if Alan Shepard or John Glenn had wimped out from the anxiety of traveling into space? Or if Rosa Parks had figured it wasn't polite to refuse giving up her seat on a bus filled with tightlipped, pasty-faced white folks?

Thank goodness there have always been people who refused to let stress stop them from their accomplishments. Wouldn't it be great to rekindle that spirit in our culture?

We could certainly use this kind of unstoppable attitude as we face an era laden with social, political, and ethical issues we haven't had to consider until now. Maybe we need a combination of Captain Kirk, Annie Oakley, and Lassie to lead the charge.

Bless You, Too

Learning to bless your stress takes you into uncharted territory, inner places you may not have visited before. It takes you closer to your core, while embracing all, not just part of what life has to offer: celebrating the good, learning from the bad, sharing failures and successes, discovering the lessons that come from disappointment, clarifying what really matters after a loss, challenging beliefs to make certain you're on target, or deepening your faith when it might feel easier to give it up.

Because stress is a natural and normal part of life, you can put your blessing on it. You can embrace it with lightness, acceptance, and wit. You can work with that excess energy instead of against it. You can teach yourself to smile instead of scowl when you feel a surge of stress because, indeed, it affirms that you are still among the lucky souls who are still actively contributing to the tax base.

It's just one small piece of the whole. When you stop and think about it, there is very little effort, energy, or thought wasted in this approach.

Chapter 2
Assess Your Stress

RUBES®

By Leigh Rubin

"I can't believe you missed the Canaan exit! ...
The next one isn't for 40 years!"

22

Chapter 2
Assess Your Stress

Let us consider that we are all partially insane.
It will explain us to each other.
—Mark Twain

Stress or Bless: There's Always a Choice

After reading this chapter you'll be better able to assess everyday situations for their stress potential. To further this purpose, we'll start out with a quick quiz. It has only two items. You have a choice between a stressing response and a blessing response: choose the reaction most typical of you.

Be as honest as you can, and if that's too difficult, read the quiz to someone who knows you well, and let them answer. Then, once you finish the heated discussion that will most likely follow their assessment, put a blessing on their comments, and read on.

Let's Play Guess Your Stress!

Situation: *You have owned and heavily used an ink jet printer for three years now. Today, for the first time, a clerk at the office supply store explains their policy: every time you return a used printer cartridge, you will receive a free ream of paper.*

You:
1.) Are ticked off because no one ever told you about this, and you can't stop thinking about all the free reams of paper you missed out on.
2.) Are delighted to hear this news, and you'll take advantage of it as soon as the current cartridge runs out.

Debrief: Yes, it would have been nice to have known

this three years ago, but you didn't have a clue about the store's policy, and hey, you were in a pretty good mood before you heard this news. Life doesn't have an "undo" button like computer software, so why let your attitude go south? You have better things to focus on, such as reading more of this book or savoring a piece of chocolate while visualizing the free reams of paper looming in your future.

Beware the Unaware

Just like the example in the quiz, you never know when a tense situation, problem person, or uncontrollable event will pop up out of the blue, like those unstoppable little ducks in a shooting gallery. Jean Paul Sartre's "Hell is other people," is probably a good reminder of what you're up against some days.

Given that uplifting statement, let's start with stranger-induced stress, wherein you are inconvenienced by those who suffer from the *I'm-the-only-person-in-the-world syndrome*. They mosey along like the Pigpen character in Peanuts, scattering little driblets of stress onto everyone in their path.

At the bank, they don't fill out the transaction slip until they get to the window; in the fast food drive-thru they act surprised when asked to fork over some cash. They sneak into express lines with crammed carts, stand and sort their letters smack in front of the post office mail slot, rush into the elevator before anyone has a chance to step out, and don't know how to merge onto the freeway. Their car radios are turned up so loud that if you're within a quarter mile, your hair and skin pulsate in rhythm with the bass line. And they shamelessly litter without giving it a thought.

In airports, they stand in an extended family cluster,

waiting for their loved one, oblivious to the disembarking travelers tripping over the welcome signs, balloons, feral toddlers, or granny's walker. When you observe these clueless types and the storm surge of inconvenience they leave behind, you can't help but wonder if they are simply ignorant of the situation or just plain dumb.

Better Ignorant Than Dumb

You've had more than your share of days when it feels as if you're surrounded by knuckle draggers. Maybe it's them, maybe it's you, maybe it's a combination of things, but there are days when you must suffer fools. Of course, just to be fair, there are days when those fools must suffer you (and your well-meaning authors, too). And just for the record, we'll define what we mean by "dumb" and "ignorant." Neither state is in any way tied to IQ or raw intelligence. Our definition is connected to attitude.

Who Knows?

Ignorance is a state of not knowing. Dumb is knowing, but not letting it make any kind of difference. For example, a person who has never watched a football game (if such an individual exists) would be ignorant of the rules. They may not get why the little guys wearing striped shirts keep touching themselves and tossing their hankies on the ground, or why the big dressed up guys keep leaping off the ground, banging their chests together.

Ignorance denotes a lack of awareness. Maybe someone doesn't know what a certain word means, or has not been exposed to a particular idea, food, culture, or activity. We all have our areas of ignorance. Yet, with ignorance, there is always hope, if someone is willing to ask, consider, and learn. If you've ever taken up a new sport, craft, or area of study, at some level you went from ignorant to educated. Maybe you learned enough to teach someone else the basics and rescue them from a state of ignorance.

Dumb and Dumber

Dumb is a different issue. Dumb means we either just don't get it or we don't want to, regardless of exposure. The old joke, "What do you think about ignorance and apathy?" and its retort "I don't know and I don't care!" pretty much sums it up. There's less hope with this condition because sometimes it's a life sentence. There are people who stick to their dumbness as stubbornly as a shopaholic clings to expired sale coupons.

Sad to say, every winter there are people who lose a few fingers after sticking their hands in roaring snow blowers to clear the blades. Others, who absent-mindedly try to repair a faulty power switch before turning off the current, find themselves going out in a blaze of glory. Of course, these are extreme examples, but dumb acts can be costly, painful, or consequential.

Of course, all of us screw up once in a while, but the dumbest among us seem to take pride in consistency. For them, it's not an isolated act, nor are they embarrassed. Maybe you've overheard a comment like this: "Dang, I can't figure out why I feel so lousy. Let me bum a cigarette and I'll buy us another shot. We can eat the rest of these chicken wings and fried mozzarella sticks while we figure out what bar we wanna hit next."

Cause and Effect: Is There a Connection?

Again, no human being is perfect, but evolution is about learning from mistakes and then avoiding them (an *oops* or *uh oh* is usually a clue). Well, you can count on being exposed to the dumb acts of others, but here's the important part. Your getting upset has very little chance of increasing the other party's competence or comprehension. For your own good, simply exit as quickly as possible before you get sucked into the vortex of their impending disaster.

You have much to bless in such a situation. You can be grateful that you are not the one burdened by such a profound lack of judgment. You can appreciate what a good story this will make the next time you entertain friends. You can feel grateful about your ability to make sound choices, and that your sense of humor can help you laugh instead of lash out at others. And when you're the one who commits the dumb act, don't get mad. Just give your forehead a light, flat-handed slap and smile. Welcome to the club!

In the Know

So what's the point? If you're ignorant about something, figure it out. Ask questions. Learn what you can. Take a class. Read about it (just like you're doing with this book). But don't be dumb. The biologist P.B. Medawar claimed that the human mind treats new ideas the same way the body treats a strange protein: by rejecting it. Not the most hopeful reminder in the world, but does that sound like anyone you know?

It's obvious you wouldn't be reading this book if you were the rejecting type. You know that good ideas can open you up to all kinds of possibilities. Hang onto that exploring frame of mind. Encourage yourself to try the new, the unfamiliar, the sensible.

Here are six stress-relieving strategies that might help:

O Listen and pay close attention to what's happening inside and around you.

O Be willing to lay your ego aside and not pretend you know something about a subject when you're actually clueless.

O If you're doing something out of the ordinary, be patient enough to think through each step ahead of time so you don't hurt yourself.

O Consciously stop and engage your brain before you open your mouth in high stakes situations.

O If what you're doing isn't working, try something new or different instead of staying in a rut.

O Safeguard your health by avoiding unwholesome habits or risky health behaviors. You know what they are.

In the words of Artemus Ward, "It ain't the things we don't know that get us into trouble. It's the things we do know that ain't so." Avoid being someone else's bad example. Admit to what you don't know and educate yourself. Next, investigate what you think you know. Be more alert, more self aware. It's one thing to be ignorant about stress and what it can do to you. It's quite another issue to know, but not do anything about it. After all, you can't bless your stress (or less it) until you've first assessed it.

No Know

There was a time when we human beings were considered the only sentient, self-aware creatures on this earth, but scientists discovered that porpoises also have an awareness of self. The study team painted different shapes on the porpoise's bodies, then turned them back into the pool where the mammals could see their reflections in mirrors.

Based on the way the porpoises lingered in front of the mirrors, swimming back and forth, looking back to front, checking out their new paint jobs, the experimenters concluded the mammals were aware that something about their bodies was different.

Have you noticed that some people seem less aware than these porpoises? A high percentage of our population has quit paying attention: look at the drivers who act as if they're the only ones on the road, hogging lanes, racing to red lights, and then lapsing into comas when the signals turn green.

Or how about the individuals who slug down caffeine all day while complaining about their sleep problems, or smokers who seem astonished that they battle bronchitis every winter?

The Price of Admission

We know a guy who popped Tums like they were Tic Tacs for years, only to discover he had a bleeding ulcer, and a woman who spent several months convincing herself that the spot on her face wasn't changing when it was. She finally gave in, saw a doctor, and had a basal cell carcinoma surgically removed. As with the twelve-step recovery programs, admission is the first step.

But awareness and admission aren't quite enough. Even knowing something is good for you isn't always enough. All of those urgings to eat your spinach because it would make you strong may not have convinced you to clean your plate. What kid wants to eat anything that green? And knowing something is unhealthy or undesirable doesn't mean you won't ever do it.

A casual "Here, have another couple of hot dogs and more pork rinds before you go," might be all the encouragement you need to exceed your annual caloric limits. If you've ever stood in a buffet line you know what we're talking about. So much for awareness! People, porpoises. Which is the higher life form?

Cell Block

Many people are blissfully unaware of the stress created by cell phone use (and abuse). Maybe you've been accosted in public by someone screaming expletives into their cell. Or you had to endure someone's inane phone conversation while standing in a line. Wherever you are, whatever you're doing, chances are good that the distracting chirp or crescendo of a personalized ring will slice through the silence. Maybe it will be your own.

Perhaps you don't know what you'd do if your cell went terminal. Yes, the device helps you stay connected with your family or work, lets you show off your personalized musical tones, do text messaging, take a snapshot, catch breaking news, retrieve your favorite team's scores, and maybe even start your car.

Cells seem capable of just about everything today except helping you floss your teeth. However, the "techno imperative"—the compulsion to remain constantly connected to the outside world—can unknowingly create an ongoing sense of urgency, emergency, and self-importance.

You've seen them, the digital cowboys of the 21st century,

packing their cells and pagers in little holsters on either side of their belts, armed to the hilt with techno bling, ready for action as they make their cross-country jaunts. With a cool glint in their eyes, they resentfully comply with the flight attendant's orders to hit the "off" button while making a last hurried pronouncement into the mouthpiece, "We're headed for Dallas." The minute the wheels hit the tarmac, these seasoned travelers retrieve their trusty cell, hit redial, and proudly proclaim, "We just landed in Dallas." as if they'd been in the cockpit, doing all the work.

Excuse us, but do you think the person on the other end of the line really cares? Has this individual been standing in "ready" position for hours, facing a massive map of the world, ready to move the push pin into a new spot? Then the documentary begins. *I'm getting off the plane now... I'm headed for baggage... I need to hit the head...* and so it goes. Now, thanks to handsfree devices, you can pop into the restroom and do your business without missing a word. Who could ask for more?

But technology giveth and technology taketh away. Whatever happened to peace or privacy? Whether you're in an airport, store, sidewalk, wedding, funeral, or theater, there's no getting away from the cell drones. They're everywhere. You've been inconvenienced, and maybe insulted by some of them just like the rest of us.

The astounding part is that they're so oblivious! The cell drones suffer from a severe social block, having no clue that they're causing stress for themselves and the rest of us. What they need is a short course in the outrageously antisocial act of *cellus interruptus*—just turn the sucker off and have a life for a few minutes!

Bonus Quiz: Are You a Cell Phone Drone?

1.) Do you find yourself beginning to panic when you only see one bar on your cell screen?

2.) Do you get anxious or secretly resentful when you are forced to turn off your cell in meetings, airplanes, or certain social functions?

3.) Do you take it personally when you see the bumper sticker, "Hang up and Drive!"

4.) Does your heart start to pound if or when (God forbid) you can't immediately locate your cell?

5.) Do you feel a slight tremor in your trigger finger whenever it gets too close to the "off" button lest you accidentally hit it?

6.) Are you plagued with nightmares about battery failures or being stuck someplace where there are no wall sockets for re-charging?

7.) If your cell doesn't ring for more than an hour at a time, do you pull it out to make sure it's still working?

8.) Do you gasp in horror when someone states that they either don't have a cell or don't use it?

9.) If technology reaches the point where cell implants are available, would you be among the first to sign up for clinical trials?

10.) Have you justified or rationalized each of your "yes" answers as you've taken this quiz?

Bonus Question: Are you peeved at us for asking you to take this quiz? Honest—we didn't mean any harm. Just hang up and read on!

Make a List, Check It Twice

Just like the cell phone drones, too many people go through their days following habitual patterns with little awareness of what's happening in their heads or how their bodies feel. It's obvious that you're ahead of the game or you wouldn't be reading this book. You already know that awareness is the first step—you must first have a clue of where your stress comes from (stress triggers) and how you react to those triggers before you can do anything about them.

Here are some questions you can use to assess your stress. We encourage you to record your answers in your Bless Your Stress journal:

1.) What things seem to bug you the most?
Note: Not fair to say "everything." Be specific. Build a list of your most common or intense stress triggers. This raises your awareness level, making you more likely to catch them before they catch up with you. Revisit this list now and then. Add new items as they come to mind or remove them from the list as you progress.

2.) Why do you suppose you get bugged by these situations: in other words, what hopes, wants, needs, or expectations are not being met?
Note: Generalizing that other people are selfish or nuts or that life is unfair isn't enough. Emphasize exactly what you were looking for and why you think this desired outcome didn't materialize. By writing out and exploring the situation in your journal you might discover ways to better

express your expectations, or more effectively adjust them toward reality.

3.) What goes on in your head when you get bugged?

Note: "Meltdown" isn't precise enough. Write down the actual words that stream through your mind because the words you use shape your perceptions. Look for repetitive phrases and extreme words (*I hate this, I'm so stupid, this is killing me, how awful, horrible, terrible, miserable, the SOB, etc.*). Pay attention to the words you think and say, and consider how they affect you. Think about the constructive words and positive phrases you might use instead.

Could you say *challenge* rather than problem; *opportunity* rather than obstacle, *inconvenient* rather than intolerable? You may laugh and say it's just semantics—of course it is! High achievers are savvy about semantics, and so are advertisers. Have you ever bought something you didn't need because you couldn't resist the lovely label or compelling description?

Face it, words sell. Looking for prunes? Some labels now feature plums because prunes just aren't considered all that sexy or desirable anymore. Fertilizer? It's evolved into crop nutrition. Hey, it's not a car, it's the ultimate driving machine. It's not room service, either; you're about to have an in-room dining experience. If word power works so well for commercial purposes, it stands to reason that the right word at the right time can work wonders for you, too.

4.) What happens to your body and your breathing patterns?

Note: Not good enough to simply say that you get stressed. Record what happens to your breathing (for example, if it gets more shallow, if you sigh, or find yourself holding your breath) when you meet up with a stress trigger.

Review what your muscles do (what parts of your body get tense or stiff, if you get restless, rushed, or disorganized). Notice how your stomach feels (butterflies, false hunger, heartburn) and what other symptoms you experience.

5.) Of the things you've listed that bug you, are they situations over which you have some control or are they completely beyond your jurisdiction?

Note: It doesn't work to toss up your hands and utter a dramatic "Whatever!" If it's something you can change (or control, even if only a little), adjust or alter whatever part of the situation you can. If there is clearly, absolutely, and profoundly nothing you can do—zip, zilch, nada, let it go, grasshopper. Let it go.

Some people haven't a clue about what they can change or control and what they can't. They have no idea how to even assess their stress, let alone bless it. Hullo! They don't recognize that they are totally and completely in charge of what goes on in their heads. Consequently, they unknowingly add to their anxiety instead of easing it.

These individuals don't comprehend that they are in possession of a mighty stress command center, powered by the greatest computer on earth—their brain.

Stay Tuned

Here's what we mean. You've lived long enough to recognize that your mind likes to keep itself busy. Think of your nonstop thought patterns as a 24/7 personal radio station, WWME. It's an exclusive all-request line, and you're both the DJ and sole listener.

If you don't consciously tune in or call in, and deliberately decide what to think about, your brain will wander all over the frequencies like an out-of-control scan button. You know how much bad news there is on the airways; there's no telling what you'll pick up.

Messing With Stress

High-stress individuals are ignorant of how they constantly set themselves up for more. They get up in the morning, look in the mirror, and mutter, "Okay, where's the SOB who's gonna ruin my day? I know he's out there somewhere!" The sad truth is, that bleeping SOB is the face looking back from the mirror.

With that kind of viewpoint, each day is simply a series of calamities just waiting to happen. A man named Jerry Bundsen has some words worth remembering. He says that you are no bigger than the things that annoy you.

Ignorance and Bliss
or
Knowledge and Problems?

Abraham Lincoln said, "If you think education is expensive, try ignorance." Consider some of the blissfully ignorant practices from a few decades ago, when people were less aware of the risks. A high percentage of physicians smoked, and many of them croaked long before their patients did.

When you're ignorant of the consequences (think asbestos or pesticides), it can be hard to grasp the connection between cause and effect. Of course, when you're just plain dumb, what difference would it make?

Okay, even though we've poked fun at it, ignorance can be risky. Of course, dumb is even riskier: consider the number of people who spend their lives with a stress level pegged in the red zone! Not that we want to worry you, but you know this isn't healthy. Pay more attention to what's happening around you and within you.

So what have we said so far? Stress is a natural, normal part of life and, to a great extent, controllable, once you recognize the symptoms and figure out why you might be reacting as you are. Consider stress as an unmistakable sign that you're still kicking, ticking, and clicking, and as far as we're concerned, this is very good news. We hope you think so, too!

We've just covered the first step in blessing your stress—assessing it. Sorry. You can't be ignorant about stress any more. And we figure you don't want to be dumb about it either.

Chapter 3
Confess Your Stress

Rubes®

By Leigh Rubin

God's factory seconds.

Chapter 3
Confess Your Stress

Everybody wants to go to heaven, but nobody wants to die.
—Earl Scruggs

You Are Unique, Just Like Everyone Else

We are all different in personality and perspective; one person's stressing is another person's blessing. Think World Wrestling Federation, anchovies, NASCAR, Barry Manilow, bird watching, online poker, and mini vans: what one person could possibly love everything on that list? Sometimes there's no accounting for taste.

This chapter will help you isolate some of the things that bug you, and ask you to admit how you may have played some tiny part in your stress. As you did in chapter two, let's start out with a quiz. Once again, identify which response would be more typical of you.

Let's Play Guess Your Stress!

Situation: *It's the end of a long and tough work week. You are eager to get home, dust yourself off, order a pizza, and relax. You're still twenty minutes away from hearth and home when you hear a radio news flash that you're approaching the scene of a big accident. As luck would have it, you just sailed past the last exit that could have saved you. Ahead of you is a string of tail lights stretching as far as you can see. As your foot moves to the brake you feel your bladder twinge.*

You say:

1.) Just my luck. I'll be stuck here for hours! Dammit! I knew I should have stayed off the freeway tonight. Stupid, stupid, stupid!

2.) Wow. This looks serious! Five minutes earlier and I might have been in that mess. Boy, am I lucky! Some poor sucker's Friday night is really screwed up.

Debrief: You can either focus on the bad luck of your minor inconvenience or the good luck of escaping a major misfortune. Discretion being the better part of valor, we pretty much figure nothing else needs to be said about this one.

Life Is Not a Duress Rehearsal

Ask parents what they want for their kids, and you might hear, "I just want them to be happy!" Yet, the United States, the most successful, envied, and imitated country on earth, rates among the highest in stress symptoms and antidepressant use. What's up with that? If our society has it so good, why aren't people happier?

For one, many of us are suffering from the "terrible too's," a social affliction that strikes the old, the young, and the in-between. Too many people are up to their eyebrows in a crammed, jammed lifestyle, pressured and plagued with too many choices, too much on their minds, too many responsibilities, too many obligations, a too long to-do list, with too little time, energy, or money in which to do it all, try it all, or buy it all.

But that doesn't prevent a lot of people from wanting it all. Few individuals stop long enough to realize that most of their complicated, complex, chronically demanding lifestyle is self-imposed. They don't realize their frenzy is the result of poor choice management. They could use Alice Roosevelt Longworth's advice: "I have a simple philosophy. Fill what's empty. Empty what's full. Scratch where it itches."

You Talkin' to Me?

Are you one of the hurried, the worried, the busy, the bugged, the dashing, the gnashing, the itchy, the twitchy, the bustling, the hustling? Do you race from one commitment to the next, draining your energy, robbing your peace of mind, and stretching your budget while still wanting more? Are you trading precious sleep and relaxation time for so-called productivity, lamenting that there aren't enough hours in the day to keep your mind and body (or relationships) in perfect shape like those relentlessly blissful people in ads and on magazine covers?

There are too many too busy, too scheduled, too-stressed, too-overworked, worked-over couples who can't stop long enough to take a breath, let alone make love or keep their relationships in shape. Now called the DINS (Double Income, No Sex), these overloaded, overwhelmed individuals find themselves frantically trying to do as much as they possibly can every day, to the point of near exhaustion.

Yet each morning, they're back out there, compulsively repeating the same frenzied pattern, as if some alien force erased their memory of the day before. They don't realize there are other options, like stop already! You might know someone who fits this description.

Sleep deprivation, budget woes, health and family issues, or worries about work add to the stress burden while nonstop advertisements and magazine articles about the Perfect Lifestyle seduce people into thinking, *Hey, I should somehow be able to have it all and do it all. If I can't pull it off like everyone else, I must be doing something wrong.*

These enticements are elaborate, incessant, and almost irresistible. Who doesn't want a model home with trophy kids and designer pets, a flashy car, great skin and hair, a trim torso, and unlimited bliss?

Resistance Is Futile

According to the ads we see on TV, miracle products or surgical procedures can make you look ten years younger, and the diet du jour will whittle you down to your perfect size. An infomercial will make you a millionaire, while an odd looking, expensive exercise apparatus will give you a buff body in only eight minutes a day. And the right shampoo will make you more attractive and maybe even happier, too.

Lurking somewhere in the back of your mind is the temptation to buy, acquire, and accumulate, lest you miss out on the opportunity of a lifetime if you don't act now. If the above description fits, come on, admit it. They say confession is good for the soul. You assessed your stress in the previous chapter, and now it's time to—well, you know. The truth shall set you free. If you are one of the stressed, pressed, and chronically duressed, take a breath and prepare to lighten your burden. Help is on the way!

Take the High Road

You've heard the phrase, "It's all in your mind." This certainly applies to stress. In the example that follows, don't be put off by its simplicity, for this is exactly how stress works when you strip away the frills. Like coming to a fork in the road, you always have a decision to make when faced with a stress-provoking situation.

And here's the piece that's critical: your decision will

be either conscious or unconscious. For that reason, stressful situations demand and deserve your full attention so that, like a smart shopper, you can make an informed decision.

We overheard a former kindergarten teacher say that a month into her retirement, after a trip to the grocery store, "My car took me back to the school instead of home." You've had those moments when you went on autopilot, right? You pulled in the driveway trying to recall whether you ran that last stop sign or actually stopped for it.

Well, it's a good idea to decommission the auto pilot. You're in the driver's seat, and when faced with a potential stressor you are required to make a turn. As they say in the Olympics, you have a compulsory move coming up, and there are two choices. You can either pull onto Stress Street or take Bless Boulevard.

You've been on Stress Street before, that meandering, seemingly endless artery clogged with anxiety, insecurity, doubt, unease, distress, worry, anger, resentment, tension, and other forms of self-torture. You've also cruised Bless Boulevard many times, a scenic byway that takes you through acceptance, peace of mind, perspective, gratitude, lightness, love, and other forms of self-affirmation.

You're at the wheel. Will it be mental pot holes or a smooth spin? You know the kind of ride you'll have which-ever way you turn. The simple truth is that you have the power to consciously choose which way you'll go and how long you'll stay on that route.

Head-On Collision or Focused Decision?

Now that you recognize it's you who makes the turn

toward either stressing or blessing, here's a checklist to keep you on track. Just as you slow down when you hit a construction zone, we invite you to park here for a few minutes, put on the flashers, grab that Bless Your Stress journal, and make some notes.

How have you been feeling lately? Has your stress exceeded the safe limit? If you described yourself as "mellow," would your family or coworkers howl in protest?

Complete any statements below that describe your current state of being so you can establish a baseline.

O   Lately, I've mostly been feeling:

__ *Harried, hurried, and hassled because...*

__ *Busy, badgered, and beat up because...*

__ *Pressed, preoccupied, and pushed to my limits because...*

__ *Tired, wired, and mired in responsibilities because...*

__ *Afflicted, conflicted, and way too restricted because...*

__ *Rested, receptive, and ready for more because...*

__ *Happy, healthy, and hopeful because...*

__ *Satisfied, gratified, and on the upside because...*

__ *Joyful, jubilant, and just having a great time because...*

__ *Blessed, blissful, and bountiful because...*

Completing these sentences gives you a stronger sense of whether you spend more of your time stressing or blessing. Are you more like a bottle of Red Bull or a cup of chamomile tea? Taxed or relaxed? Whether the process is conscious or not, stress is a choice. The point is so simple it can easily be missed. This is the time to come forward and confess your stress so life can take a turn for the better.

Your Turn

Yogi Berra once said, "When you come to a fork in the road, take it." We say take the high road. Making the shift to blessing your stress is not as tough as you might think (hint: anything you have learned, you can unlearn and relearn). After all, you are in charge of what goes on in your head: remember that "all me, all the time" 24/7 radio station WWME. You have the power to switch the channel or change the programming. Stress or bless—it's your call.

Check Your Mental Baggage

Stress can't be measured in inches or pounds, but a lot of people haul around a hefty load of stress wherever they go. The problem is, they don't realize it. Maybe you don't realize how much stress you cart around, either. Imagine having mandatory *Stress Security Check Points* stationed here and there, complete with uniformed guards who would require you to pass through *Mental* Detectors (no, that's not a typo). Imagine being scanned with Attitude Wands (like the ones they use in airports to detect metals and other forbidden objects), only these wands would check for what's weighing down your mind.

Nothing would escape detection with these highly sensitive devices. Hidden grudges, resentment, anger, worries, rage, envy, anxiety, and other forms of smuggled self-sabotage would sound the alarm. You'd be required to locate these items and leave the emotional contraband behind. Imagine what life might be like if you were wanded every day before leaving your home or upon arriving at work.

Imagine the mutual "I told you so's," or "Aha! I knew it!" if spouses could "wand" each other! But do you think your daily travels might go more smoothly if you lightened up your load of mental baggage? Only one carry-on allowed per trip.

Light or heavy? Up or down? Good or bad? Simply put, there are optimists and there are pessimists. The optimists seem to travel lighter. They have a mystifying resilience. When something happens, they deal with it and bounce back. But things are more weighty for the pessimists. They seem more stressed, more easily brought down. They find it harder to let things go. If the latter statement describes you, then you're a candidate for frequent scans with your own attitude wand. Make it an essential daily ritual so you can travel first class.

Irks, Jerks, and Quirks: What Stresses You?

Stress. It's as commonplace as cell phones at restaurants, malls, and meetings. And everyone has their own list of what bugs them. When we ask people what causes their stress, we get a hot button roster so long it could stretch to Jupiter and back. Here's a sampling:

Family, bosses, coworkers, fast drivers, slow drivers, complicated technology with miserable documentation, vacations gone bad, high gasoline prices, high-priced low-quality products...

People who interrupt, cut in lines, talk too loud, know it all, babble on their cell phones in public places, carry on conversations in movie theaters...

Spoiled kids (your own), spoiled kids (other people's), bad food, food that tastes so good you can't stop eating it, barking dogs, uppity cats, tamper proof caps only a child can jimmy...

Crying babies and feral children in fancy restaurants, people who are always late, people who are always early and expect you to be on time...

Rude service personnel, rude customers, surly strangers, self-important smokers who treat the world like it's one big ashtray, militant nonsmokers who get in a huff over one puff...

Drivers who don't use their turn signals, those who drive for miles with their turn signal blinking...

Restaurant servers who ignore you, those who burden you with their life story between courses...

Clerks who don't count out change properly, people who cough on your money or food before they hand it to you, and more. We could fill a book!

You get the point: just about everything can cause stress if you let it. Please humor us for a moment and go back over this list and count the situations you complain about most often. Smile to yourself and think of the potential energy wasted over these awful inevitables. How absurd to let a potentially good mood go sour over something you can't control!

In the Mood

Okay, we admit it. With so much stress potential out

there, sometimes it's hard to keep your perspective. Like a Big Mac Attack, a bad mood can pop up out of nowhere and take over your impulse control before you can say, "extra sauce."

The next time you feel your stress begin to spike, imagine that if you don't curb your attitude, you'll end up stuck in a long line filled other cranky customers hellbent on having a lousy time. You don't need that Snappy Meal! Opt for the Lite Mood menu instead by asking yourself the following calming questions:

Is this a small, medium, or large annoyance? Note: super size is not an option.

In the long run, am I better off blowing up or blowing it off?

If this is a big deal, how stressed should I get and how long should I stay that way?

Asking these three questions can help keep your blood pressure low and your self-control high. Maybe you've never asked yourself these kinds of questions before. Maybe you've just reacted because you didn't know there were other options, or you simply didn't take time to think about it.

Write those three "calming questions" on a piece of paper and carry it with you. Or if you'd like an official version of the Calming Questions Card, send a self-addressed, stamped envelope to *Bless Your Stress*, P.O. Box 956, East Lansing, MI 48826, and we'll be happy to send you one.

Whenever you feel your attitude begin to veer toward the bad mood drive-thru, pull out the card and read it. Pause.

Think about what you want to have happen. Consider the potential consequences of your actions. Then take a nice deep breath and smile. This short break in your routine might be all you need to lighten your stress load a quarter pound or so.

Asking logical, calming questions can stave off anger outbursts and keep you in a rational frame of mind. In fact, if, for some reason, you were unable to read the rest of this book for awhile, this single strategy could make a significant difference for you.

Step and Turn

Star Trek's Mr. Spock is the perfect role model of a logical, rational mind. Spock would work through the who, what, where, when, why, and how of a situation before making any kind of decision. You get the idea. Use your logic and intellect for problem solving rather than allowing yourself to be driven by emotion or impulse.

Just like in twelve-step programs, admission is the first step—and the turning point—in the recovery process. This being the chapter on true confessions, it's time to pony up, admit, and move on. That's great progress in itself, but please be patient.

It took some time to get where you are on the stress charts, and it will take a little time to turn yourself around. There's no magic potion to make your stress go away: no frog to kiss, no super hero to make it dematerialize, no Ouija board to consult. Stress is energy, and you have the power to redirect its force. But first you have to identify old habits that have allowed that energy to run amok inside you. Only then can you realize your "bless" potential.

Your Habits Become You

Benjamin Franklin described time as the stuff of which life is made, and the same applies to habits. If you have ever embarrassed yourself or gotten into trouble thanks to force of habit, you would agree that unconscious behaviors (nail biting, excessive throat clearing, constant complaining, to name a few) can complicate your life and contribute to your stress.

Well, stress reactions (impatience, anger, intolerance) can become so ingrained you simply go there without thinking, like a default setting on a computer. You can't manage those moments until you're fully aware of them.

To help you better identify and address your potential stressors, here are three items to explore in your Bless Your Stress journal:

1.) List one common triggering incident that tends to boost your stress level. For the record, a stress trigger can involve any person, situation, or circumstance that has the potential of pushing your buttons.

For example, one of your authors (hint: Leslie) needs to consciously keep herself composed so she doesn't come unraveled when dealing with hoses that twist and tangle. Your other author (hint: Mimi) needs to deliberately keep herself in a nonjudgmental frame of mind so she doesn't get irritated with people who are late for appointments.

2.) Identify your most common response: how you might tend to lose it in this situation, or in some way add fuel to the fire. Determine exactly how your actions intensify your stress.

Imagine for a moment the usually calm and contained Leslie straining and cussing, madly yanking and jerking a twisted hose instead of systematically working out the crimps. Or the usually genial and friendly Mimi checking and rechecking her watch, getting more exasperated with each passing nanosecond instead of sitting relaxed and un-ruffled, waiting for her friend or client. All right, we've confessed some of our sins, now it's your turn.

3.) List the symptoms that typically indicate your stress level is surging. Examples: a familiar shot of adrenaline in your gut, instant feelings of extreme impatience, aggression, or helplessness (a desire to strike out, throw something, yell, and so on).

You may occasionally find yourself smack in the middle lane on Stress Street without even realizing you made a turn. Well, you have to know exactly what you're doing before you can modify a habit. The more familiar you become with your stress triggers, typical responses, and symptoms (as outlined in these three steps), the easier it will be for you to read the signs and address potentially stressful situations. Sorry. We can't do that for you. We're still working on our Psychic Network skills.

It always pays to examine your unique perspective and identify your expectations so you can pinpoint your major stressors—situations that have the potential of setting you off. By writing about these circumstances, you'll not only raise your awareness, you will also figure out better ways to cope.

Journaling helps you tap into your innate wisdom, which is always waiting there around the corner, curled up on the rug, wagging its tail, ready to be called in for action and adventure. By addressing your stress issues clearly and candidly, you'll be more capable of better controlling the forces within you and around you.

The Question of Control

Speaking of control, this is an issue for all of us. Count how many times you've heard people explain, "...but then, I'm a control freak..." Those who balk at setting foot in airplanes or resist medical procedures that require anesthesia are quick to explain that they "don't want to give up control."

Just about everyone likes to think they're in control most of the time but sorry, this is pretty much an illusion. Even when you have the remote in your hand, if there's someone else in the room, you may not have as much control over what gets watched as you'd like to think.

For starters, you have no control over the forces of nature, other people's driving habits, terrorism, the world economy, famine, pestilence, what people say behind your back, what happens to food that sits in the refrigerator for too long, the genetic deck you were dealt, or how your hair or complexion will look on a given day.

Yet, people back seat drive when their spouse or kid is behind the wheel, wear their lucky tie, and hang a good fortune totem on their car rearview mirror. They freely express their opinions, judge the actions of friends, family, or strangers, and get snarky about the weather. They tsk and sigh and condemn or disapprove, acting as if they alone have access to some mystical button that controls the universe.

And then there are the well-intentioned but controlling parents who not only attempt to protect their children from potential perils (and rightfully so), but also try to rescue them from experiencing the inescapable childhood letdowns that build character. If you've fallen prey to any of the above, we hate to burst your bubble, but give it up.

Life: the Ultimate Reality Show

Life is quite a ride, don't get us wrong. It's just not all that controllable and you'll feel more blessed and less stressed once you accept this bite of reality. People say they enjoy reality TV because it's unpredictable, but the story lines are well mapped out. You want spontaneity? Get fully immersed in your own reality. Give up that imagined dominion over all those things that will happen regardless of what you do, and get on with the things that really count.

Focus on the things you truly can control: what you think, what you say, what you feel and do, what you put into your mouth, and what you do to your body. It's an alarmingly short list, wouldn't you say? This is a point worth remembering.

Maybe you're familiar with the universal principle which states that you cannot truly have something until you first give it up. Well, here's your chance to fully and completely embrace your life, and you only have one tiny thing to give up—the control you never really had.

The Official Control Release Form

I, _____ do hereby waive and relinquish my unofficial and ineffective hold on the forces of the universe. From this day forward I shall refrain from trying to control people, events, the weather, and other circumstances that exist outside of my personal domain.

In recognizing that my responsibilities do not extend into

the intergalactic realm or even into the next county, I shall culti-
vate restraint, foresight, wit, wisdom, humor, reverence for life,
and a healthy regard for reality. I accept my new, more limited
life role with full recognition that the universe will continue un-
folding as it always has, without my clumsy and completely su-
perfluous attempts at intervention.

*Date*_____

How Do You Spell Relief?

Now that you've taken the control release pledge and relinquished your imaginary control over just about everything, we invite you to heave a deep sigh of relief. Think of all the extra time you'll now have! Maybe you'll even sleep better, knowing you no longer bear the awesome burden of universal responsibility. Your step will be lighter, your mind freer. Who knows what you might be able to accomplish now that you're liberated from those weighty cosmic responsibilities.

It's a big step, and for this leap of faith you'll get something back. A good deal, actually: more peace of mind, a broader perspective, and maybe even more patience, for starters.

Once you leave your stress-producing patterns behind, new doors will open. And in case any of those bad habits sneak back in when no one is looking, the next two chapters will help you hand over their walking papers so you can stress less and bless more. You've taken a big step: you've confessed your stress and faced the reality of what control really means. You'll find more good news in the chapters that follow.

Chapter 4
Address Your Stress

"I can't believe it ... here we are, living in eternal paradise, and all *you* can do is complain that the mattress is too soft!"

Chapter 4
Address Your Stress

Turnabout Is Fair Play

Happiness isn't always getting what you want, but wanting what you get. In this chapter you'll explore how you add to your stress burden or ease it. You'll recognize ways you unknowingly hinder your attempts to create a meaningful life, and discover simple methods for paring down some of life's complications for less stressing and more blessing.

Sometimes We Get In Our Own Way

If you've ever learned a physical skill (softball, skating, golf, tennis, knitting, cooking) you probably remember the early phase when you were painfully mindful of the proper technique. You may have felt very self-conscious as you concentrated on each separate step, trying to perfect your form.

Eventually, though, with practice, it all became second nature—muscle memory took over and you didn't have to think so much. If you ended up taking advanced lessons, you probably found yourself going through the entire process all over again, only at a higher level.

Life follows a similar pattern. The learning curve is steep when we're young, curious, and craving to learn about the world around us. Just think of the endless, exhaustive questions little kids ask. But by the time they reach high school, there are few questions asked anymore—peer pressure, boredom, and restlessness replace curiosity. By the time many kids graduate from high school or maybe college, the desire to absorb new information seems to radically drop off.

While there is always much to learn, great numbers of people, at some point, figure they pretty much know everything they need to get by in life. We say yes and no to that. Yes, there's always a lot to be learned, and no, who wants to just get by? You never want to stop learning. That you are reading this book puts you in an elite category; the average citizen is lucky to read a book a year.

Huh?
There are people who are so casual about learning (okay, lazy) that they pay little attention to what goes on around them, including their own actions. Take, for example, those who think they can make the elevator come faster if they repeatedly push the button. Or the drivers who try to hurry slow trains by honking their horns. These individuals are clueless about how they're contributing to their stress.

But hey, it's not always a snap to figure this stuff out even when you're paying attention! Habits are easy to build and hard to break. Human nature being what it is, there's a tsunami of unconscious stress swirling around out there. This chapter will help turn the tide. But first, here's the quiz.

Let's Play Guess Your Stress!
Situation: *After years of driving used cars, you are finally in a position where you can buy your first brand new one, all decked out to your specifications. It looks great and drives great, and it feels terrific cruising around, inhaling new car smell.*

But when your prized possession is only three weeks old, a seventeen year old boy panics while trying to make a left turn, and bangs into you. No one was hurt, your car wasn't totaled by any means, but right now the grille and front bumper look like you've been in a demolition derby. Two days after the altercation a friend says, "I'm sorry to hear about your accident."

You say:
1.) I can't believe my luck. My first new car and what happens? Some idiot kid who needs a brain and two years of driving lessons ruins my car! Of all the beaters I've owned, why did it have to happen now? No matter how well the dealership repairs my vehicle, it'll never be the same!

2.) Hey, it's just a car!

Debrief: Maybe in an ideal world this wouldn't have happened, but it did. Unfortunate experience or outrageous insult? It's up to you. You can't "unbang" your car, but you can keep your outlook intact. After all, it could have been worse, right? No one was hurt. Your car can be repaired, but if you or that young man had suffered serious injuries, you could have had a real tragedy on your hands. This is called perspective, and it's a great trait to cultivate.

If you didn't choose the second item in this quiz, relax. We're not going to send you back out on the road for a guilt trip. Of course, it would be disappointing to see your new car get smashed, even if the damage were minor. You'd have to go through the inconvenience of dealing with the insurance company and renting or borrowing a car while yours was in the shop. You'd have some out of pocket expenses to contend with. But there is one small blessing: no longer would you have to endure the suspense of obsessing over when you'd get that first scratch or ding. Bygones!

Life is Complex

Granted, life is filled with complications and inconveniences (the insurance paperwork connected to an accident and the required repairs are two examples). Jumping back to reality, you are living in complex times. Every day you have to reckon with concerns about work, family, health, money, global instability, and whether you've got a good shot in the Lotto this week.

If you feel at all uneasy about life's uncertainties, you're justified. The world you live in is much less predictable and far more volatile than it once was.

In our culture for example, people are more outspoken about what they want and don't want. They're more adversarial and more insistent about their voices being heard above the rest. In a time when cooperation and collaboration are critical, the political climate has instead become more contentious. Go figure!

And yet, in both the blue states and the red states, life somehow manages to go on. Despite the edgy external environment, in your personal life you still experience moments of joy, closeness, and celebration, and may these good times of yours go forth and multiply.

Studies of human behavior reveal two circumstances that make us all squirm: uncontrollables and unpredictables. Scan the evening headlines and you'll find a handful of both categories—small wonder we have our moments of unease. But in the last chapter, you signed the official form that gives up your fictitious hold over the things you can't change or control. Your life trundles on in spite of these realities.

A big picture perspective will help you adjust your viewpoint so you can feel more passionate about the people you love and life as you live it. You could call that a blessing, by the way.

A Meaty Subject

Given our current climate, it's obvious that life isn't as simple as it once was. Take something as mundane as meat handling. The consumer warnings on meat packages today read like the labels on *Weed B Gon* or plutonium, admonishing us to thoroughly wash our hands, utensils, and anything else coming in contact with the contents of the package.

Imagine the moms of yesteryear making meatloaf for dinner, fingers blanketed with particles of raw meat, merrily wiping the baby's nose, buttoning buttons, refereeing disputes between warring offspring, answering the phone, peeling potatoes, tossing the salad, and so on. These days, we're browbeaten into cautionary practices rivaling the protocol of a world-renowned surgical team before we cook. Small wonder we feel stressed, even in the privacy of our own homes!

Please Pass the Whine

And then there's party planning. Have you had friends over lately? There was a time when having a party meant buying a case of beer, buns, a giant bag of chips, and slapping together a pot of sloppy joes. But today it's a different story: you need to accommodate the special food needs and preferences of everyone you invite, bless their demanding, self-absorbed little hearts.

You now have to please the meat eaters, the junk food lovers, the vegetarians and vegans, the ones who call themselves vegetarian but will eat fish when no one is looking, the drinkers, the non drinkers, the sulfate reactive, the gluten allergic, the lactose intolerant, the chemically sensitive who insist you send out an All Points Bulletin that no one must show up wearing fragrance of any kind, those who only drink bottled water, those who won't touch it, and those who bring their own provisions because they only partake of clean food and pure liquids.

To appease those who insist on a semi-sterile environment, have some anti-bacterial soap on hand, too. But after conforming to these exhaustive, obligatory measures, who's in the mood to celebrate?

Fed Up

We interviewed a corporate meeting planner about Eater's Entitlement, and triggered a rant. It seems that people flaunt their dietary needs and preferences not just in their personal lives, but at work, too. Our source told us that at company functions, people get snappish about what is or is not included in the corporate spread.

Rather than brief the food committee ahead of time, they lurk on the sidelines until the big day, and then irately recite the litany of everything they can't eat, as if their food sensitivities were documented in their personnel files. One woman marched up to our whistle blower and wailed, "Look at all these donuts! I can't touch them. How could you not know I'm diabetic?" Well, we do now. And we just found out a whole lot more about you, too.

There was a day when food complaints were simple and predictable. "It wasn't all that good, but I ate it anyway." Granted, there are still a few holdouts—those who frequent buffet-style restaurants don't seem so hung up about what they put in their mouths, or how much. As we've said before, one person's stressing is another one's blessing.

But Don't Panic

Okay, so life is isn't always simple or seamless. But there's no need to panic when things don't go the way you want. In the long run, you'll feel better if you can savor the sweet victories and roll with the punches, hang onto the good, and let go of the bad.

Yeah, we know, this sounds like a cheap made-for-TV-movie where the frazzled coach tries to fire up a faint-hearted batter approaching the plate, but it's true. You can't control everything in life, let alone predict it. Why waste precious energy fussing about annoyances and irritations?

You're the only one who suffers from this time-wasting activity. So take down that "BANG HEAD HERE" sign in your office and swear off the stewing. You don't need any more self-inflicted wounds. Patch yourself up and move on.

In the past, yes, you had your moments where you lost it. But there were also times you kept yourself calm and cool in the face of adversity. Which worked better for you in the long run? Too many people overreact to situations and then have to pay the price, mentally and physically.

From now on, practice positive procrastination: *don't go into panic mode until you know you it is absolutely necessary.* You'll save a lot of wear and tear on your body and mind, and maybe some of your relationships, too.

Here's a way to remember this important lesson.

Place your finger on the circle you see below. Press and release. Then repeat the process one more time.

What happened? If you said nothing, you're right. You could push on that puppy all day long, and nothing will happen. What you just pushed is the panic button, and guess what. *Nothing ever happens* when you push the panic button because it isn't connected to anything! We hope that the next time you're tempted to push the you-know-what, you'll remember this little demonstration of how completely futile it is.

Normal? Who You Callin' Normal?

You probably know a few people who have taken panic button pushing to Olympic levels. They worry, sigh, tsk, judge, envy, complain, and produce enormous quantities of stress. They rush around, stuck in warp speed, worrying and obsessing over little things from dawn to dusk, multitasking, exhausting themselves, suffering fitful sleep night after night.

Suggest to these busy bodies that they sit down and relax, and they'll look at you as if your hair is on fire. *I tried relaxing once,* they say with a faraway look in their eyes. *But then I started thinking about all the things I shoulda been doing instead of sitting there like a lump, so I quit.*

Ask how long they lasted and they say, *I dunno. Maybe three minutes.* They then explain that if they hadn't gotten up and done the things they were itching to do, they would have ended up feeling ten times more agitated than before they sat down. These individuals put no stock in relaxation. It's too stressful.

Then there's the other extreme: people who are so laid back you want to stick a mirror under their noses to see if it fogs. As Groucho Marx once said, "Either this man is dead or my watch has stopped!" and sometimes that's how it feels.

These easygoing individuals can sit without reading, eating, knitting, working on their to-do list, talking on the phone, or watching TV. They don't hurry and aren't annoyed if someone's late because they're usually the ones not on time, and who's keeping track anyway? There are few darned emergencies or crises for these types, even when the contractions are two minutes apart. It's all just life, and they only have one speed.

What's Normal for You?

For the two styles we've just described, their behavior is normal. For them. What's normal for you? The following statements will help you identify your everyday patterns and behaviors and determine how they affect the quality of your day.

O Typically, the first words I hear myself think or say in the morning tend to be:
__ *more stressed because...*
__ *more blessed because...*

O For the most part, in my daily life things tend to:
__ *tank shortly after I slide out of bed because...*
__ *remain fairly level and free of frenzy because...*

O Generally, my daily commute:

__ *tends to set me off and put an edge on my day because...*
__ *tends to be laid back and enjoyable because...*

O Mostly, my waking hours are:
__ *crammed with multitasking, stress, and high speed activity because...*
__ *pretty laid back with relaxation time and breathing space because...*

O Mostly, I would describe my attitude toward work as:
__ *stressful and unrewarding because...*
__ *satisfying and fulfilling because...*

O Overall, I would describe the important relationships in my life as:
__ *conflicted and chaotic because...*
__ *satisfying and supportive because...*

O Typically, by the time my head hits the pillow at night I feel:
__ *tired, wired, and close to expired*
__ *ready for a good night's sleep*

O Generally, I would describe my life right now as:
__ *having had better times than right now because...*
__ *pretty happy and healthy because...*

Complete each of the above statements as candidly as you can in your Bless Your Stress journal. Addressing your stress requires knowing yourself and your everyday behaviors, and recording your thoughts will give you a concrete means of measuring your progress. Don't panic if your answers leave a bit to be desired; just pick one item and work on it for awhile. Be sure to take whatever time you need to work on yourself.

So far, there exists no *Extreme Makeover Stress Edition* TV show that offers instant relief. But, chances are, you'll still be kicking two or three months from now and you can do a lot about your stress issues in that time.

A Drastic Measure

Speaking of measurements, after reading this sentence, take a moment to place your hands on your ears. Now draw your hands forward, holding the same position, and study the distance in between. You have just measured the size of your stress triggers. From the isolated incident to how you react to it, the entire process takes place between your ears.

Yes, that miraculous, busy brain of yours is the keeper of all you've experienced, from your earliest memories way back in the dark ages, to your most recent insight. Your mind is filled with thoughts, feelings, beliefs, values, perceptions, prejudices, expectations, and more.

Whew! That few inches between your ears is the exact distance between a potential stress trigger and its outcome. You can either take your finger off the trigger or squeeze and shoot.

So, what's a stress trigger? It can be a person, incident, or even information. Not everyone responds identically to the same triggering event. It's you who ultimately pronounces it a source of stress or something to bless. Skiers, for example, love hurling themselves down a steep, slippery, mountainside while less hardy souls might prefer watching TV or dusting.

Some riders love galloping cross country on their horses, jumping fences so high neither can see the hill, water hazard, or downward slope waiting on the other side. The less physically inclined might prefer reading, flossing, or napping as their favorite pastime.

Inside Edition

Your perception of what constitutes fun or fulfillment in your life may be quite different from that of your family members or coworkers, or even your best friend. Perception is the key. Odd as it may seem, even the same situation can prompt different responses in you, depending on how you're feeling about things at the moment. Here's an example: *Imagine that, within the span of an hour, two coworkers tell you how good you look today. One of these individuals you like a lot and the other you don't.* Compare your reaction in the first instance to the second one and how you might interpret each individual comment. Same situation (trigger), but what made the difference? You!

T.I.E. One On

Remember how we measured the stress trigger? Well, that remarkable distance between your ears is the center of your stress factory, where your stress is either produced or reduced. Aren't you a marvelous, multi-talented creature! Rather than allowing yourself to get all tied up with stress, you can T.I.E. one on instead. Here's how this three-step process works:

1.) "**T**" stands for Triggering event *(in this case, a comment made to you)*.

2.) "**I**" represents your Internal reaction *(the judgments and evaluations that go on in your head—whether you consciously* *or unconsciously decide to stress, bless, or stay neutral).*

3.) **"E"** signifies your External response *(your behavior—what you end up saying or doing).*

T is for Triggering Event

All triggering events (people, places, or experiences) get processed in your brain. The problem is that most people don't take the time to separate one step from the next. They leap from the first step to the third without realizing that something very important happens in between. The next time you're faced with a potentially stressful situation—a Triggering event—stop!

I is for Internal Reaction

The second step (Internal reaction), is the one that will make the difference. Consciously sort through what's going on in your head. Review exactly how you are interpreting this situation. Note whether your mental process is rational or emotional, proactive or reactive, objective or skewed.

Just think; here is something in life you can control, if you wish. You are always the ultimate source of stressing, blessing, obsessing, or second guessing any stress trigger that presents itself. Stay tuned to what is going on in your head—how you are interpreting the situation—and the next part will almost take care of itself.

E is for External Response

After your self-evaluation, make a conscious decision about what you plan to say or do—your External response. Focus on trying to achieve a beneficial outcome. By consciously working through these three steps you'll stay more clear and calm, and avoid slipping into defensive reaction mode. You will handle sticky situations more effectively.

Memorize the **T.I.E.** steps and work through them whenever you're presented with a stress trigger. You'll be able to consciously and deliberately choose more appropriate responses.

To help make this "lesson" stick, you will want to take a little extra time and return to your Bless Your Stress journal. Recall and analyze a recent stressful incident from the **T.I.E.** perspective:

1.) Briefly describe the Triggering event (what happened).

2.) Explain your Internal reaction (how you evaluated or interpreted the event and why).

3.) Describe your External response (your reaction, exactly what you said or did).

After you record the outcome of the situation (step 3, External response), consider how you feel about it. Given what you now know, could there have been a better result? Think about what might have happened if your Internal reaction (step 2) had been more deliberate.

Yes, that middle step is the pivotal decision making point. If this seems hard or bothersome, don't worry. You're in the process of building a new skill, and just as we described in the opening of this chapter, things may feel weird or awkward at first. You may feel a little self-conscious, but that's a normal part of working on a new skill. With a little bit of practice, the unease will go away and your new way of thinking will become second nature.

Take a Moment

Working through—that is, learning—the **T.I.E.** process is not a blow-off exercise. We're asking you to do this because what happens at step 2 (your Internal reaction) is often unconscious and spontaneous. And it happens at warp speed. You have to consciously stop the action and mull things over before you can figure out how you are evaluating and interpreting a triggering event.

This takes practice; you may not be crystal clear as to exactly what goes on in your head when you're faced with something stressful. Few people are. Maybe, like others, you've often just reacted with little or no thought and then had to hose yourself down afterward, awash in the consequences of your actions. But now you can do better than that. Way better.

If Knot Now, When?

Some people believe life should never be inconvenient. Others believe they deserve a better life, and that wonderful things should happen to them (winning the Publishers Clearinghouse Sweepstakes, losing ten pounds in a weekend, finding a bag of large, unmarked bills), regardless of how little effort they've invested. That kind of arrogance and entitlement guarantees a few knots in the stomach, for sure!

Granted, you may have had moments like that, but the feeling passed quickly. You know the rewards of doing your inner work or you wouldn't be reading a book like this. Once you regularly use the **T.I.E.** process, you'll unearth some personal beliefs that cause you to become frustrated, disappointed, or even desperate. You'll also discover untapped reservoirs of inner strength and discipline you didn't know you had.

When you **T.I.E.** one on, you'll not only reduce your stress load, and raise your self-awareness to new levels, but you'll think more clearly about the outcomes you want and what it will take to achieve them. You'll change how you regard yourself and how you relate to others. This three-step process has the potential for significantly altering how you think, feel, and behave.

Step 2, the *interpreting* process, is the essential step in learning how to think more rationally and less emotionally. As you know, your emotions blur your reality. Your feelings can get in your way, causing you to construct your own unique (and often inaccurate) version of what's going on.

Oscar Wilde wryly stated that the advantage of emotions is that you can get carried away by them. But the disadvantage is that you can get carried away by them. Truth be told, when you keep your feelings moderated, you can interpret your experiences more objectively. This means you'll be better able to analyze a situation and evaluate your behavior more clearly and rationally.

Mind Over Matter

Remember the early Star Wars movies, and how young Luke Skywalker had to replace his fear with The Force before he could receive the power to fight evil. Luke had to put himself in a rational, objective, and open frame of mind to let The Force come to him, be with him, empower him.

While for you the outcome won't likely be as dramatic, nor the background music as sensational, you can simulate the essence of Luke's experience. Rather than trying to force a situation, you can create your own empowering *force* of calmness and rationalism instead.

Thinking in a rational mode doesn't mean you'll start acting like an android or that you'll have no feelings, nor does it mean you will stifle your emotions. It means you'll be more capable of separating fact (objective observation) from fiction (emotional bias). It means you will be more clear, more centered. You'll think things through before you respond, and the choices you make will be far more suitable than the knee-jerk outbursts so common today.

Trying To Be Right
Can Sometimes Make You Wrong

At no time are our emotions more raw than when dealing with a conflict or difference of opinion. Recall a recent disagreement or argument with someone you care about. Each of you came to the situation with your own perceptions, beliefs, and feelings. If things escalated, it's because neither of you could get past your emotions and into a rational frame of mind.

To understand these dynamics more clearly, listen in on someone else's conflict when you can (we guarantee you'll be more objective). Chances are, both parties will think they're right, and just to complicate things, each of them will have some valid points. Each of them may end up trying to make the other person wrong, even if things worked out okay.

You could even hear a last accusing comment from one of the parties as their "discussion" winds down. "Well, this was **almost** a disaster thanks to **your** making us late!" We know a couple who, for years now, travel to the airport separately and meet at the gate when they go on vacations, to avoid this very scene.

It truly is the little things that make a big difference. We ask you never to forget that little distance between your ears and the immense difference it can make. With deliberate thought and practice you can perfect this powerful, life-changing skill to the point where the three-step **T.I.E.** process kicks in automatically.

Shift Happens

If a book could feature a drum roll or strains of spirit-stirring music, this is where we'd interject the pomp, for this single idea (**T.I.E.**) could be a turning point for you. Learning the process, internalizing it, and putting it into practice was indeed a turning point for both of us. It may be the hardest task we will ask of you.

We can't stress strongly enough that the effort is so very worth it. We hope you'll take the ideas in this chapter to heart and that what we've offered here will help you address your stress by making a shift in the way you think. Every day, you'll bless yourself for having made the effort. We do.

Chapter 5
Less Your Stress

RUBES ®

By Leigh Rubin

Calendars in hell

Chapter 5
Less Your Stress

You have to live life to love life,
and you have to love life to live life.
It's a vicious circle.
—Source Unknown

It's All About You

Earlier in this book we suggest (okay, emphasize) that while the world abounds with potential stressors, it's you who picks up and fills out the stress requisition slip. You are your own stress factory, and the level of production is your call.

The ideal is to keep output at a level where you're happy, healthy, and not feeling hassled most of the time. This way, you feel pretty capable of handling whatever life tosses at you: no creeping anxiety, shortness of breath, chronic worry, nervous stomach, festering anger, raging impatience, or emotional hot buttons that propel you into the stratosphere.

If those symptoms sound extreme, they are—but look around and you'll witness all kinds of people suffering to the extreme because their stress mills are stuck in overtime mode. You've been inconvenienced or even insulted by some of them while waiting in lines, driving your car, or shopping.

To help keep you from joining this pack of people behaving badly, in this chapter you'll visit the inner workings of your personal "stress manufacturing plant." During the tour, we'll give you what you need to scale back production for good. But here's the first official stop: the quiz.

Let's Play Guess Your Stress!

Situation: *You enter a public restroom, walk into the only available stall and witness an impressive display of waterworks all over the seat. Apparently, someone was either in a big hurry when they staged their visit, or their aim was very poor. Granted, it's not like you're going to plop down on a public toilet seat, stake your claim and move in, but this is a pathetic leave behind (no pun intended).*

You:

1.) Tsk and sigh at the endless capacity of human beings to vent their secret parental resentments by defiantly not cleaning up after themselves in public places. You stifle a secret desire to wring the slob's neck over this lack of consideration for others.

2.) You recall a humorous piece of graffiti you've seen scrawled on the inside of stall doors: "If you sprinkle when you tinkle, be a sweetie, wipe the seatie."

Debrief: This slightly gross situation is one of the many impositions you can potentially face on any given day. Will you let it throw you? The reality is that you'll find all kinds of stressors out there, and neither wishing nor whining can make them disappear. If you want to keep lightness in your life, you can't let yourself get dragged down by the awful inevitables.

In fact, when you are able to cleverly sidestep the stress connected to what's wrong with the world (think bombastic talk show hosts or doggie piles), the more time and energy you'll have to bless what's right in your life (think fragrant flowers or a loved one's smile).

And now, here's our version of being a good citizen when

using public restrooms (or private ones, for that matter).

If, in the course of doing your job, you wet the seat, don't be a slob. Just give the spot a friendly swipe so no one else will have to gripe.

A Clean Scene

The above is a trivial issue, to be sure, and one that is easily forgotten. But there are somber circumstances and serious incidents that will be hard for you to let go of. From minor inconvenience to major injustice, certain things will stick, especially if they directly affect you.

Thanks to 24/7 global bad news reports, even some remote events (ethnic cleansing, natural disasters, airborne illnesses) can be unnerving and hard to shake.

The world is full of concerns, misfortunes, and distractions. It takes a strong will to shake off details you can't do anything about. For keeping your mental slate as close to a nonstick surface as you can get, let's borrow an example from *felix domesticus*, the common house cat.

If you've ever owned a cat, you know they are the ultimate groomers. Imagine the commercials if there were a cat channel! Tabbies spend hours preening, cleaning, licking, flicking, fluffing, buffing, swiping, and wiping themselves so they look fresh, pressed, and presentable for their admirers. But there's a price to be paid for all this upkeep.

Every few weeks or months, if you're around at the right moment, you can witness the results of all that hygiene. Enter the hairball, a mysterious, moist wad of foreign material your kitty efficiently produces and spits up with a flair.

The Urge to Purge

Just as in the world of our beloved pets, we human beings have a lot of hygiene and maintenance duties. Some of it just happens, some of it we have to work at. Every day, our body automatically sloughs off cells, bacteria, hair, and foreign particles. Similarly, we regularly dust, vacuum our homes and cars, brush our teeth, clean our nails, and swipe at our belly button lint or ear wax.

We're pretty good at the outer hygiene, but who teaches us about inner clean up? How about brain lint or mind wax, the residue of the stressors that collect over time? For a moment, imagine a single day in your life and all the potential irritations you're exposed to.

Now reflect on how they affect you and how you typically handle the residue from those situations. Do you consciously expel those single strands of stress, or do you unknowingly let them collect into a wad of worry and anxiety?

Humans and Hygiene and Hairballs—Oh My!

Maybe you're wondering what cats and hairballs have to do with you. Think mental hairball. What if you could preen, clean, and hygiene your mind the way cats do their fur? What if you could collect all your stressful, unsettling thoughts into a soggy glob and cough them up?

Metaphorically, we think this is possible and recommend you spend a few minutes a day purging the mental hairballs before they collect into a mass so big you could choke on them. Here's a handy rule for the stressful remains of the day: *when in doubt, spit it out.*

Help for Hurling the Hairball

You're probably familiar with the Heimlich Maneuver, the quick, effective rescue method for dislodging objects caught in the esophagus. Many a choking person has been saved by this technique, and there's even a way to Heimlich yourself.

We invented our own technique to prevent the formation of mental hairballs. Now, in the midst of a stressful day, in the privacy of your own home (or office) you can restore a sense of calm and inner peace with a technique we call the "Heim-like Maneuver." It's doctor approved and requires no special training to apply:

Sit quietly for a moment. Shut your eyes and gently place your hands on your diaphragm with your thumbs touching the point where the Heimlich would be administered. Behold your beating heart. Smile just a little bit and take a moment to appreciate yourself (that's the "like" part of the Heim-like).

Take a deep breath, pause for a couple of seconds, and then slowly exhale. Relax your face, your jaw, your shoulders, your thighs; anywhere you may feel tension. Feel the rhythm of your rising and falling breath and the cadence of your heartbeat. Let a wave of stress leave your body with each exhale.

Once you establish your breathing rhythm, slowly drop your hands into your lap for more relaxation. If you believe in cosmic consciousness, bless yourself on every inhale, and with each exhale, send your blessing to the needy souls of the world.

Stay in this position for at least two minutes, longer if you can. Feel yourself calming down. Hard to believe, but research shows that brief periods of stillness help you feel less stressed and more blessed. Your heart rate slows, tension leaves your body, your mind regroups, and you shift closer to your center. Your energy quietly reorganizes. You both relax and recharge.

Who would think that such a simple gesture would have so much power? You can Heim-like yourself several times a day, whenever you feel the need. It only takes a couple of minutes, and the benefits last for hours. You won't ever need a prescription, and there are no unwanted side effects.

Now Hear This

Years ago, leaders of the emerging health food movement coined the phrase, "You are what you eat." Well, how about, "You are what you think." May we be so bold as to ask, just how do you think—what kinds of thoughts fuel your brain?

Mental junk food includes negative thinking, worrisome, angry, or resentful notions, jealousy, greedy fantasies, dread, dissatisfaction, or visions of retribution. High performance brain fuel involves positive thinking, optimistic anticipation, appreciation, affirmation, generosity, openness, satisfaction, or hopeful visions.

Adrift in Oceans of Notions

We're harping on the issue of paying attention to what goes on in your mind because your brain suffers from the "idle hands are the devil's playmate" ethic. It wants to stay busy, really busy! Remember the people who can't sit still for three minutes because they start thinking about all of the things they could be doing if they weren't sitting there trying to think about doing nothing?

Your brain, like everyone else's, is constantly occupied, thinking both deep and shallow thoughts, playing and re-playing songs you both love and hate, drifting in and out of daydreams, recording unusable trivia and factoids, fretting over things that have happened, worrying about things that might happen, conjuring up stuff that never happened (nor could ever happen), judging the actions of others, and strolling down memory lane. Your stress plant doesn't want to go out of business. It just can't help itself.

Does this sound familiar? To some extent, everyone suffers from this condition, and once in awhile you will notice that your thoughts get carried away. It starts with a simple notion that all of a sudden jumps on the mental merry-go-round for a gazillion revolutions, around and around, and over again. We named this condition *Repetitive Notion Syndrome* and no one is immune.

A Not So Sweet Refrain

Imagine the following: *You had a rather unsettling conversation with your (boss) (spouse) this morning, and hours later you're still feeling a bit jarred about it because things were left on a sour note.*

As if you don't feel bad enough about the way things went, you now turn to station WWME for the hand wring-ing hour so you can feel even worse. Instead of rationally analyzing what went on, you replay the worst parts of the interaction a few hundred times.

Once you tire of that self-torture, you start embellishing and playing out all kinds of detailed scenarios that didn't hap-pen, some that couldn't possibly happen, and a few you wish *had* happened. Then you repeat each story line a few hundred more times in case you don't feel bad enough already. As a friend of ours says, "It hurts so good, quit it some more!"

It's not enough to obsess over recent events. You can also punish yourself by dredging up transgressions from the past, as if repeating these upsetting moments again and again can somehow magically alter the course of your history. Your inventive, restless mind just doesn't know when to quit. But you can stop this absurdity. You have the ability to switch the station, make the mental shift, and play a better tune.

Build up your resistance to repetitive notion syndrome. It's debilitating to expose yourself to such unnecessary strain, pain, and energy drain. You have better things to do with your time, like figuring out how to open that bottle of vitamins with the tamper-proof cap or clearing out the dust bunnies lurking under your stove.

Speaking in Tongues

Words hold tremendous power. For example, depending on where you live, you might occasionally have to cope with cockroaches. Or Palmetto bugs. While the latter might seem like less of a pest, the awful truth is that both the city slicker and semitropical resident are family. Indeed, they have the same last name.

When estate tax became the death tax, what are the chances it morphed into something different—or better— just because it had a new name? It's hard to imagine that any fat content was lost when Kentucky Fried Chicken resurfaced as KFC. Ah, words.

Sweetbreads or organ meats? Tripe or intestines? French fries or pomme fritte? So, what's in a word? Plenty! Think of racial slurs, dismissive phrases, cruel nicknames. Compare "Snow White and the Seven Dwarfs" with, "Young virgin held captive in isolated cabin by mutant cult members." Pay attention to the words you use, whether you're talking to yourself, or others. They have a constant influence on your stress factory, whether you know it or not.

Think of the billions of dollars corporations spend each year on advertising and marketing campaigns, or the money made by spin doctors for crafting just the right political message. What about the catchy jingles or phrases you can't get out of your mind from commercials that haven't been aired for decades?

These mindless pieces pop into your head, and you're stuck with them for the rest of the day. Out of respect, we have chosen not to include any such gremlin here, lest you be plagued with it for the next twelve hours.

But it's not just ads or jingles that stay with you. Within your mind you carry an aggregate of words and phrases that influence you, especially messages from your childhood. Maybe someone you respected once encouraged or inspired you by saying things like, *You're really good at this... You are such a good reader. I hope you go to college... You are a gifted athlete... You are extremely talented...*

But perverse creatures that we are, negative comments often hold more weight than the positive ones. An offhand criticism or harsh statement from a parent, teacher, sibling, or friend can have unsettling staying power. Some statements are hard to shake: *You're not college material... You'll never amount to much... Why can't you be more like your (brother) (sister)... You're just trouble. You always have been!* In a flash, you not only remember what was said, but you relive all the feelings from that very moment as well.

Thanks for the Memories

All of this old stuff is buried deep within your memory bank, and it can take on a life of its own. A lot of what you were told about yourself as a child was either off the mark or dead wrong—and now that you're grown up, it no longer applies.

But sad to say, it's easy to tap into those early messages and play them back. Many seemingly well-balanced adults are perpetually hounded by ancient, irrelevant, often debilitating opinions and assessments. And just so you know, this is a natural human tendency.

To some extent, mental recall is something everybody does, only some just don't know when to quit. As for you, there might be something stored in your memory bank that has lasted to this day.

What dominant messages did you grow up with? Take a moment to review some of the words that influenced you early on in life, both good and bad. Some of them may have been the sources of your early stressing (or blessing). The following questions are worth mulling over in your Bless Your Stress journal:

O   What specific themes or messages did you most often hear as a child? Write them down.

O   How have these messages or themes influenced your attitude, belief system, and self-appraisal, even as a grown-up?

O *When you screw up or make a big mistake, how do you talk to yourself? What old messages come back in full force and gang up on you?*

O *Make a list of any old messages you need to discard: the negative or discouraging ones that no longer apply to you as an adult.*

O *Make a list of the encouraging, empowering messages you heard early on in your life: ones you want to hold onto, ones that continue to bolster your confidence or self-esteem.*

O *Write down a new self-affirming statement that connects to who you are now: words you can use to reassure yourself in personal or professional situations when you need inner strength or encouragement.*

If you weren't able to immediately answer any of these questions, don't worry. Just mark this page and come back to it after you've had time to think about things. In time, your recollections will percolate to the surface. You'll be able to record those words or phrases and evaluate their long-term influence on your behavior. Always remember: it's never too late for a personal makeover.

Unthinkable Talk or Unsinkable Talk?

Let's switch back to station WWME for a moment and check the talk show schedule. Because your brain is constantly talking to you, it pays to truly *hear* what your internal station is playing. Are your mental air waves filled with stressing thoughts or blessing thoughts? We cannot emphasize enough the importance of paying attention to your inner dialogue and changing the programming when needed.

Imagine your stressing thoughts as "unthinkable" self-talk. Hanging onto negative notions and unconsciously repeating those self-defeating patterns thrusts you into a downward spiral that diminishes your sense of self. Unthinkable self-talk fosters helplessness, hopelessness, displeasure, and defensiveness, to name a few.

"Unsinkable" self-talk, on the other hand, represents a form of self-encouragement that fortifies your confidence, buoys your determination, recharges your energy, and feeds your spirit. Our point is simple. You must first recognize and acknowledge which of these thinking patterns are more typical of what goes on in your head. You can switch the station and find a new talk show—if, indeed, a change is in order.

Your thought process is the key to how you see the world. You carry within your head a data base filled with beliefs, perceptions, biases, impressions, values, judgments, experiences, and more. You filter virtually every experience through your data base. Everything you believe about yourself, other people, and the world in general has a tremendous effect on your perceptions.

Do your everyday thought patterns tend to be unthinkable or unsinkable most of the time? Consider which of the patterns listed below are more common for you.

The Unthinkable: Stressing Self-Talk

This is awful and horrible, and I simply can't handle it...

Just my luck — I knew something dreadful would happen...

This absolutely makes me crazy...

How could you do this to me...

This (can't) (shouldn't) be happening...

I'll never get over this...

I can't do this...

The Unsinkable: Blessing Self-Talk

This is really a tough situation and I'll have to work hard to handle it...

This is not at all what I wanted to happen, but I'm not in charge of the world, only myself...

I absolutely refuse to make myself crazy over this...

I know other people's bad behaviors say more about them than they do me...

I don't like what is happening, and I need to find a constructive way to deal with it...

This is one of the toughest things I've ever had to deal with, and I need to take good care of myself...

I'll give it my best shot and be prepared to accept whatever happens...

Next, the Subtext

One of the first things you'll notice is that most of the unsinkable (blessing self-talk) statements are longer than the unthinkable (stressing) lines. That's because they are original, rational, and non-emotional. They're also active and self-affirming.

You could label the unthinkable (stressing self-talk) as part of a weary, dreary script borrowed from a drama queen character in a badly written soap opera: commonplace, hysterical, exaggerated. It takes no effort to dredge out any of these overused hack phrases from the sorry lineup of "pity party" lines we've heard all our lives. The subtext says, *I'm a victim. The world sucks. I'm just going to sit down, wring my hands, wallow in self-pity, and give up before I hurt myself.*

But unsinkable self-talk is different. It's unique, optimistic, rational, and custom designed to fit the situation. Blessing self-talk constitutes the distinction between being controlled by your emotions or controlling them. Think of the possibilities! Making the transition from "poor pitiful me" to "cool capable me" is an exciting process, and it takes some work.

With thought and practice, you can reframe your outlook, reshape your perceptions, and rebuild your belief system. The subtext of unsinkable self-talk goes like this: *I can handle this if I keep myself calm and fully present in this situation. I have both the ability and desire to bless rather than stress if I so choose, regardless of the outcome.*

Alas, human nature being what it is, you may find that it's terribly easy to lapse into unthinkable self-talk. The problem is that without your realizing it, victim-based thought patterns and repetitive notion syndrome can become a habit.

Like a puppy chomping on a chew toy, your brain grabs onto a negative thought, replays it a thousand times or more, and spins you into a stress cycle. Well, guess what: you can stop the action, write yourself a fresh script, and rehearse those new lines to give yourself more peace of mind.

Show Up for Rehearsal

What we're saying is, if you're going to play or replay thought patterns in your head, why not make sure they have bless potential instead of stress potential? The minute you catch yourself grabbing onto a fretful, angry, or worrisome thought, stop!

Just like flipping a switch, consciously replace that negative, nagging dialogue with constructive, encouraging words. Halt the action whenever you catch yourself thinking something like:

Omigod, this is just killing me...

This so totally sucks—I am completely devastated...

I'll never get over this. My life is ruined...

I can't stand this...

Your brain can only hold onto one thought at a time. Force out the emotion-sodden, unthinkable self-talk with calming, encouraging words. Remember the chomping puppy example and give your brain a better toy to chew on.

Wait a minute. I'm letting myself get all upset over something that hasn't even happened—I don't want to do that to myself...

I have a lot to feel grateful for in my life...

What a waste to focus on one tiny thing that's gone wrong...

I don't like this at all, but I can handle it if I try...

Your words frame your perceptions, interpretations, and expectations. *Emotional words and stressing self-talk have the power to bias, constrain, and contaminate your judgment, making you vulnerable to stress and frustration.*

Your perceptions, which are based on your belief system, can prevent you from seeing things as they are. They only let you see things as you are. Rigid beliefs about what life should be like—or should never be like—are a perfect setup for stress.

Maybe you can't fully bless every situation, but you can jettison that stress with the power of your mind. Unlearn your old stressful patterns and learn your new dialogue. Teach yourself a series of positive statements designed to banish the negative ones. Rehearse your unsinkable self-talk lines until they become second nature.

Act Up

So what are we suggesting? The next time you catch yourself dragging out a limp, languishing, overly dramatic line, cease and desist! Consciously shift into blessing self-talk mode. Don't let yourself get away with a theatrical hand-to-brow-poor-me dialogue.

You're better than that, and you deserve a better quality script. You don't have to sell yourself short with unthinkable thought patterns. Imagine the potential blessings once you take charge of what goes on in your head.

Only you can revamp your inner dialogue. Only you can update the WWME play list. There's no one else in the control room. Take advantage of the few things in life you can actually control!

Chapter four and this chapter, too, deserve rereading. This is the application portion of the book. We hope you'll revisit these chapters many times and complete the exercises in your journal. Spend some quiet moments reflecting on how these ideas can help you and the first steps you need to take.

Your active involvement is essential because simply reading isn't enough. Knowing isn't enough, either. Knowledge only becomes wisdom through action. In other words, it isn't what you know, it's what you *do* with what you know that makes the difference.

New View, New You

Objective, rational thinking can liberate your world view. It can offer you a more open and emotionally honest way of looking at things. The first step is to investigate your perceptions and challenge your assumptions for accuracy. Are you working off old data or current information? As you explore your beliefs, values, biases, and experiences you'll more clearly understand the connection between your perceptions and feelings, and how your thoughts influence your feelings (and vice versa).

Putting this all together takes some time, but it can also unleash a cascade of insights you might otherwise never experience. The time is perfect for you to venture forth in this pursuit, and the ideas in this book will support you every step of the way.

With a little bit of effort you can infuse yourself with an unlimited supply of self-encouragement. Just for fun, call it the "iProd." Think of it as a tiny mental device you can carry with you at all times to stay motivated. Create and download your own play list, turn up the volume when you need to, and repeat as often as you like.

We offer this handy device because prodding yourself to take the first step toward personal change is the hardest part. It takes confidence and self-assurance to try new ways of thinking and behaving. But you can do it. The iProd is yours to use as you see fit. You can less your stress by making these good ideas part of your everyday life.

It's For You!

Your mind is the key to what you see, and what you say about what you see.

The words you use create mind pictures.

Mind pictures help shape your belief system.

Your belief system connects with your emotions.

Your emotions drive your actions.

Your actions create consequences.

You use words to evaluate how you perceive the consequences.

And the cycle starts all over again.

It's all about what goes on in your mind.

The lines can be unthinkable or unsinkable.

It's all about your language.

It's all about you.

Chapter 6
Yes Your Stress

RUBES ®

By Leigh Rubin

leigh 6-21

www.rubes.com

Creators Syndicate, Inc.
© 1996 Leigh Rubin

Rubes® cartoon © Leigh Rubin - Used with permission

Samson's plan hits a snag.

98

Chapter 6
Yes Your Stress

I try to take one day at a time,
but sometimes several days attack me at once.
—Jennifer Unlimited

Don't Obsess—Just Say Yes

Some people refuse to accept stress as an inescapable part of life, but just like the air you breathe, it's all around you, and ranting or complaining won't change a thing. Blessing your stress is about anticipating its ongoing presence and inevitability.

After reading this chapter you'll probably agree that many of your stressors aren't really all that awful; they're just inconvenient or mildly irritating.

As you incorporate what you read in this book, instead of blaming or looking for a scapegoat, we hope you'll be more inclined to take the 3-R approach:

Revise your outlook, and
Revamp your reactions, so you can
Rebound from life's annoyances and awful inevitables.

While we're on the topic of such things, here's the latest quiz.

Let's Play Guess Your Stress!

Situation: *You're exhausted and wrung out after traveling all day. Having survived two late flights and indigestion from the lousy airline food you had to pay extra for, you arrive at the hotel where you'll stay for two nights. All you want is to check in, shower, and collapse into bed so you'll be fresh for tomorrow's conference. But alas, it appears that your reservation has gone missing. You have a confirmation number, but the clerk says it doesn't match their system. You know you called the right hotel because the phone numbers match up, but the clerk is unmoved by your evidence.*

You:
1.) Blow up and vent your day's frustrations at this dense desk clerk who seems way too dim-witted to be trusted with sharp objects.

2.) Heave a sigh and consciously decide to suck it up. Facing the person who is in charge of your short-term destiny, you take a breath, collect yourself, and with forced patience, ask how the situation might be resolved.

Debrief: After enduring this scenario enough times to make our own travel version of the movie *Groundhog Day*, we, your much traveled and sometimes unraveled authors, acknowledge that it's awful being hit when you're down.

No, this kind of snafu should not happen, but it does. No, you can't do anything about what happens before you get to that fateful registration desk, but yes, there are things you can do once you're standing there.

This kind of inconvenience isn't a huge issue, really, in the bigger scheme of things (street crime, corporate corruption, cellulite), but it feels like a big thing. You're tired and out of your element. The air travel system controls your time, food options, and physical space. You reach your destination worn and weary, yearning only for privacy and recuperation, but sometimes you have to pay a price.

The price is controlling your compulsion to be right. You may be right, but flaunting it can hurt you. Focus on the results you want: a quiet room where you can kick off your shoes and grab the remote, maybe even raid the mini bar. Here's a lesson we both had to learn the hard way: *Why alienate the person who is in control of the kind of room you end up with, or whether you even get one at all?*

The Way Things Go

Where is it written that life will be perfect or you will be the only person on earth exempt from annoyance, irritation, or even occasional anguish? The human spirit is both amazingly naive ("This shouldn't happen to me!") and resilient ("We shall overcome!").

If or when awful things happen to you, chances are you will somehow summon the strength, faith, and inner resources to cope with, and in some cases, triumph over adversity. But this book isn't about tragedy or major loss. It's about the needless stress you impose on yourself when you let too much of the small stuff get in the way. This book is about the potential blessings you might miss when you take your focus off the big picture.

Little things can quickly build to a boiling point: that long line you have to stand in when you're in a hurry, the permanent stain on your favorite outfit, a sluggish computer, a copier that keeps jamming, the pokey driver in front of you who appears to be doggedly headed for the same place you're going. Things will happen, objects will break or spill, mistakes will occur, people will do dumb things. That's how life on this planet goes.

Your existence is filled with dynamic tension. Good and

bad. Yes and no. Push and pull. Up and down. Life is all of these things and more. Say yes to this simple truth, smile the next time you're faced with one of life's speed bumps, and like on the TV game shows, you'll advance to the next level.

Lessons or Lesions?

Life is chock full of what we like to call "Everyday Informal Education: Insightful Opportunities" (EIEIO). When faced with a touchy situation, irritating circumstance, or annoyance, chances are good you will either walk away with some kind of lesson (usually about yourself) or mental lesion (usually self-imposed).

Instead of getting mad, call it an EIEIO and ask yourself, "Where's the lesson here?" then stand by so the answer can come to you. Don't litter your mind with judgment, *This person is an idiot,* or dismissal, *Whatever!* Stay focused on what you can learn about *yourself* instead.

Look for the expectation that didn't get met, how you would have liked things to unfold, and figure out why you didn't get what you wanted. Look for different ways of handling things for a better outcome next time. Remind yourself that little annoyances can grow into big stressors. This is especially important if the situation seems oddly familiar.

Is this something you've struggled with before? Hey, do you figure that if this situation has once again resurfaced this might be a lesson in itself? By now, you know the drill: if what you're doing isn't working, try something different.

Take nagging for example—we all do it, but don't want to admit it. Now and then you probably nag someone about something you either want—or don't want—them to do.

Let's say you'd like your spouse to quit smoking. Every time you bring up the subject, you get excuses and defensive reactions. Your "discussions" become shorter and more heated (relax, we've all done it). But instead of giving up the habit, your spouse becomes less communicative and more sneaky about grabbing a smoke.

Bag the Nag

Maybe, just maybe, there's a lesson here about the effectiveness of nagging as a method of persuasion (not that this stops a lot of people). But take down those black lung posters you hung on the bedroom wall and that smoking cessation brochure you taped to the bathroom mirror. Instead, try writing a note, not about the smoking, but about how much you love your partner. Then back off for a while and see what happens.

When you want or expect people to change, they often end up feeling that they are wrong and you are right. This puts you in the superior position (hint: think parental), and chances are, you'll get resistance. It takes time for the other party to sort things out, work through the issue, come to terms, and admit a change is in order. It's very difficult for someone to change when they are being watched.

When you can back off and provide some "emotional space," you increase the chances of getting the outcome you're hoping for. Of course, we're discussing everyday annoyances and minor issues that interfere with enjoyment of life and those we love. If your situation is extreme, such as alcoholism or a gambling addiction, seek professional help.

Yes Your Stress

Life is not perfect. Irritations and annoyances will happen. Things will go wrong. On the day of an important presentation or interview, your hair will look awful, or Mt. Zitsuvius will erupt in the middle of your forehead during the night. If your pimple is really that big, call the *Guiness Book of World Records* and maybe you'll qualify for the next edition.

All right, we know. Life is sometimes uncomfortable, inconvenient, or embarrassing. It's not funny now, but it could be—some day off in the distant future.

Go ahead and chew on some of those inevitable slices of reality that are waiting to be plucked and popped in your mouth. Accept that you will be abundantly blessed with little or big challenges almost daily. When you're in a hurry, expect that you will be surrounded by dim-witted, dawdling drivers and long slow lines, or temperamental technology. Count on it that the moment you hit "send," you'll catch a mistake in your vanishing e-mail.

Anticipate that the minute you decide to lose weight, your appetite will double. Accept that little things will go wrong. After all the times you've been assailed with aggravations, why should you still be surprised or indignant? You know better than to turn minor incidents into emergencies—expect the glitch, hitch, or stitch, and smile when they happen. For once, you get to feel smug about being right!

Edith Wharton once said that if only we'd stop trying to be happy, we'd have a pretty good time. And any time you want, you can use life's dynamic tension to maintain inner equilibrium. Think of the high wire walker in a circus act who defies the law of gravity through a delicate blend of balance, focus, and practice.

Living with a tendency to bless rather than stress calls for the same qualities. To resist or protest the inevitable is to violate the tenets of your Official Control Release Form. When you lose it over an inescapable inconvenience or annoyance, you shatter the intricate balancing act of simultaneously applied tension (effort) and relaxation (accepting and letting go). Better to stay in "the zone" and maintain your balance.

Don't Resist, Persist!

Saying yes to stress requires a new way of thinking. That's what the previous two chapters are all about. Your words affect the size of the stress load you carry every day, and if you want your perceptions to change, you need to change your language.

This isn't a snap. It's human nature to cling to old habits. Just like the example of the high wire walker, making a mental shift requires simultaneous effort and letting go. The transition from unthinkable to unsinkable self-talk requires unlearning old habits and learning new ones. If you've ever tried to stop smoking, quit caffeine, or give up sugar, you know how hard it is to change a habit.

Back Talk

As you practice your new self-talk (I *can* instead of I can't), your brain will talk back, forming excuses and protests: *Oh yeah? What makes you think you can do this? You've never been able to do it in the past!* or *This is stupid and you're stupid for even trying. It won't make any difference at all.* There's been a lot of talk in recent years about the "inner child" but who talks about the "inner brat"? Well, you have one. So does everybody else.

The inner brat is balky, bullheaded, sullen, stubborn, rigid, and relentless. It's your inner brat that will wheedle and protest when you try new, self-affirming behaviors. Expect this resistance. Prepare for it. Persistently repeat your new thought until you hush that tiny, whiny inner brat. Funny, isn't it, the things we say to ourselves. We'd never tolerate such back talk from anyone else!

To make this practice stick, turn to your Bless Your Stress journal:

1) Focus on one situation in which you are trying to replace what you consider a bad habit with a better one.

2) Write down your new unsinkable self-talk statement: an "I can" affirmation you will memorize and repeat when a stress surge starts.

3) When your brain starts back talking, write down what you hear from your inner brat. Neutralize these protests by repeating your encouraging, unsinkable statement over and over again.

4) Make notes on your progress from week to week as your inner brat backs off. It won't take long for the little monster to give up and go take a nap.

Life Equals Learning

Life is all about learning. As a child, you sought and embraced life's captivating lessons. You were driven by curiosity. But as an adult maybe you got a little jaded or bored, and copped a "been there, done that" attitude. Perhaps your opinions hardened. Consequently, you may have found yourself resisting new information.

It's no surprise; consider how often you've heard people

say, "You can't teach an old dog new tricks." And maybe when you've tried to have a heart-to-heart discussion with your spouse or lover, he or she barked, "Don't get into my head!" or something similar. Some people don't want to learn. They want things to stay the same, even if they're not terribly happy about it. Go figure!

Yet, learning is instinctive, even life-giving. Think of the lessons you've learned about sheer survival from dumb mistakes or near misses. Think of the insights you've gained through the years that help you truly connect with those you care about. Think of the health-related information you can access today that may help you live longer and be healthier. Be consistent and persistent about learning: it's one of the purest instincts you possess.

Following Your Instincts

All babies are blessed with pure instinct. A newborn instinctively knows to seek and suck on a nipple for food, or cry when it has a need. A baby bird instinctively knows to leave that safe, warm nest and take its first, shaky flight into the huge unknown. A tiny fawn knows to sit perfectly still, rather than flee on shaky legs when danger approaches.

These are profound examples of pure instinct. You, too, were born with pure instinct. It serves you well, protecting you from danger, guiding your judgment, and inspiring your love. But of course, it's not that simple.

Instinct Versus Impulse

Instinct is just that: it's hard wired, intuitive, instantaneous. But there's also a learned response you want to be aware of—one that doesn't serve you so well. Call this adaptive impulse; it's a self-protective set of patterns you learned early in life from experience. You developed these secondary reactions so you could conform, please, or appease others, shield yourself from judgment and criticism, or avoid getting into trouble.

Think about how instinctively honest a child can be (*Grandma, how come you have so many wrinkles?*) and how unacceptable this is. Driven by the desire to be liked, loved, or appreciated, most of us learn to replace pure instinct with adaptive behaviors that are more socially acceptable so we can avoid punishment or rejection. After all, many adults consider children who speak their minds inconvenient or bratty. Timid, overly sensitive, or extremely curious children are called scaredy cats, cry babies, or snoopy, respectively.

When you were a child and subject to adult judgment, maybe you learned to stifle some of your honest reactions because they weren't acceptable. You conformed to avoid punishment or blame. Small wonder children learn to cover their tracks with adaptive impulses—who wants to get in trouble all the time or be grounded until they're thirty?

Mastering Your Impulses

Adaptive impulses can cause you to second guess yourself and everyone around you. Instead of owning up to a mistake, you may be tempted to blame someone else or fake innocence. Adaptive impulses include omissions, lies, deviousness, defensiveness, manipulation, and other insecure reactions.

Any time you consciously attempt to alter your story, cover your you-know-what, or justify any less than honorable actions, you're probably chugging along on the low octane fuel of adaptive impulse.

As you become more self-aware, you'll recognize when you're slipping into adaptive impulse mode. You'll be able to stop yourself before it's too late. Try to be a purist. Call upon your pure instincts whenever possible, but you'll find this doesn't always come naturally. Old fears and insecurities will get in the way. It's probably occurred to you that adaptive impulse contributes mightily to stress and unease because of the inner conflict it creates.

When you find yourself in a dicey situation, a part of you may want to own up. But your impulse to cover up or protect yourself from the consequences of your actions may be far stronger. Resist the temptation. Try the opposite tack. Suck it up and do the honorable thing. Be responsible. Or as some say, "response-*able*."

An Opposite Approach

Blessing your stress doesn't come naturally (if it did, we wouldn't have written this book). It isn't hard wired. In fact, this approach is the opposite of what you've been taught about stress (handle it, manage it, control it). Blessing your stress is like a gentle mental martial art that requires practicing distinct skills and strategic "movements" until they become second nature.

In Aikido, for example, students must learn to do the opposite of what comes naturally. If you signed up for an Aikido class, you would be taught the offensive skill of moving toward your opponents, not away from them, to gain an advantage. You'd learn to override the inclination to back off or move away, and instead, step into your opponent's space to effectively defend yourself. This method takes practice to perfect because it's the opposite of what you think you should do.

You've often heard that the best defense is a good offense, but we are not naturally inclined to move toward our stress. It's more our nature to move in the other direction: to deny our anxiety, to try and escape its influence, or to blame someone or something else for causing it.

While logic may tell us that denial, escape, or blame won't work and may actually invite additional stress, we don't necessarily buy it. The bless option is a *learned* response that requires practice, and it's as effective as a well-rehearsed Aikido move.

No More Duress Rehearsal

And now let's do a quick review. In practicing the mental martial art of blessing your stress, you are training your brain to behave in a new way, and at first it may not want to cooperate. In order to change and control the thoughts that go on in your head, you will need to practice your unsinkable thinking the same way you would a new physical skill: repeat it over, and over, and over again.

Initially, your brain won't know what to do with your radical script rewrite. It will feel clumsy, awkward, and unnatural for a while. Old habits are hard to break—but not impossible. Expect that your brain will at first resist your new way of thinking.

The first time you switch off the WWME soap opera "poor pitiful me" show and tune in to the "cool capable me" program, expect resistance. As you state your new phrase, perhaps an encouraging, *I can handle this!* your inner brat may spout off, *Oh yeah? You've never been able to handle this in the past!* or *Who do you think you are—Braveheart? Gimme a break! You're more like Chickenheart!*

Remember the mental martial arts training: go to the mat and move closer to that contrary, resistant inner voice. Repeat your unsinkable self-talk statement. Say it every time your inner brat balks at your new behavior. Remind yourself that you're in the middle of a transition, and this inner turmoil is only temporary. Eventually your new self-affirming lines will win out. Building this new habit is definitely worth the work.

Regaining Control

By now you grasp the theme of this book: there are only a few things in life you can truly control, and most of them dwell within you. You signed away your personal hold on the universe a few chapters ago.

But you've been compensated by discovering that you are in charge of what goes on within your very own "youniverse," the vast, mysterious world that exists between your ears. Learning to monitor your thoughts, emotions, and impulses should be enough to keep you from raiding the refrigerator for at least a few hours.

In case you'd like more support in your quest for less stressing and more blessing, we are pleased to offer you a handy, dandy low tech but high performance device—your very own multifunction *Personal Control Panel*. It's simple to operate, ready for installation, no remote necessary, no batteries required. Learn the functions of this indispensable portable unit, and take it with you wherever you go. Just push the appropriate button as needed, and you're in business. It's so simple, even an adult can master it without needing to be rescued by a techno whiz kid.

Your Personal Control Panel

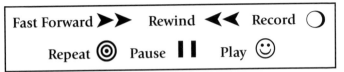

Quickie Instruction Manual

If you're like most people today, you've been stuck in **Fast Forward** for years, chronically rushing, hurrying, hustling, speeding, and multitasking, while still falling behind. Well, stop! Breathe. Relax. We hate being the bearers of bad tidings, but you'll never get ahead of the time curve.

Maybe you've heard the old expression, *The hurrieder I go, the behinder I get.* For your convenience (and relief), we have disconnected the **Fast Forward** button. We agree with Ghandi, who said there had to be more to life than seeing how fast you can get through it. Take heed: the answer is not speed.

Use the **Rewind** button sparingly. This function works best for situations requiring alertness, self-awareness, and judgment. Use Rewind when preparing for a substantial discussion with your spouse, an important work presentation, or critical interview. A cautionary note: don't let the Rewind button keep you focused on the past or bogged down in the *if only, shoulda, coulda, woulda* disorder. Brief Rewind episodes are best.

Similarly, be selective about what you **Record**. File the best, get rid of the rest. In other words, consciously choose what gets stored in your mental warehouse. Author Rita Mae Brown says that happiness only requires choosing to have a short memory. Retain the good experiences and consciously discard the bad ones; don't get hung up on negatives or uncontrollables. This will put you in a frame of mind where there's less to get stressed over and more to bless. Imagine how happy this will make everyone who lives or works with you!

As a rule, you won't need the **Repeat** button too often, unless you're trying to memorize something or practice your new unsinkable thinking skills. Punch the Repeat button too often and you may fall victim to repetitive notion syndrome or ineffective nagging patterns; you don't need either of these in your life. We repeat: you don't, you don't!

But the all-purpose **Pause** button is an entirely different matter. Wear the print off this one! Whenever you're faced with a stress trigger, push **Pause**. Stop, draw in a deep relaxing breath, and take stock. **Pause** before you lapse into adaptive impulse mode and say something inflammatory. **Pause** before you react to that high testosterone driver who honked at you. **Pause** before you tell that snippy service clerk or gossipy coworker what you really think.

Pause before you go bananas over a long slow line or traffic jam. Take a moment and chill. You get the point: use it (the **Pause** button), or lose it (literally). Pushing **Pause** keeps you hovering a few extra moments in the present. It gives you one more chance to relax and regroup before you take action. It's the "stopportunity" of a lifetime—the **Pause** that destresses!

And then there's **Play**. We hope you'll wear the finish off this button, too. It's been said that we don't quit playing because we grow old, we grow old because we quit playing. You can't feel terribly stressed if you add more play to your life. You'll definitely feel more blessed, and so will the people around you.

Play it Again: A Review

You don't have to live your life stuck in **Fast Forward** mode—let this button stay on permanent disconnect. Why rush and mush and miss so much of the game?

When you slow up your pace, you have a better shot at gaining full understanding of what's really going on inside and around you. You're more likely to access your pure instincts and the wisdom you've gained through experience. You not only end up with time to smell the roses, you might even be inspired to plant some, too.

Without an occasional **Rewind**, you might shortcut your history or rob yourself of reflection time (more learning), so use this button as needed. And then there's **Replay**. Thanks to human nature, there's a tendency to recall more bad situations than good, so if you're going to push this button, make it a good memory, or a purposeful one.

If and when any potentially stressful situation raises its gnarly little head, push **Pause**! And make full use of the **Play** button every day.

Well, that's how your Personal Control Panel operates. Instead of unconsciously letting other people push your buttons, consciously and knowingly push your own. See, there really are a lot of things you can control!

Who needs intergalactic supremacy when there's so much to be done within your inner space? Your own little "youniverse" awaits your exploration. Say yes, and go where few have dared to venture. You'll bless yourself for being so bold.

Chapter 7
Finesse Your Stress

RUBES®

By Leigh Rubin

"Excuse me, sir, but I believe
you were supposed to lead us to
the land of milk *and* honey?"

Chapter 7
Finesse Your Stress

Oh Lord, help me to be pure, but not yet.
—St. Augustine

Yin and Yang

Life comes with its own special sets of stressors, just like salt and pepper, peanut butter and jam, Minneapolis and St. Paul. Not just living, but loving involves stress, sometimes truckloads of it! We fall for someone new, fresh, and different, but later on those same attributes can make us grit our teeth.

Our source of joy turns into a source of woe. In all areas of life, from hobbies or competitive sports to intimate relationships and even parenthood, we sometimes bless—and stress—over the same activity.

A lot of people think that life is all about wanting and getting. But in the long run, do we always fully appreciate getting exactly what we want? TV's Murphy Brown once complained that children must be God's way of punishing us for enjoying sex. And Henny Youngman lamented, "What's the use of happiness? It can't buy you money!"

Talk about yin and yang—what we do for fun can sometimes send us into a funk. Hobbyists and athletes participate in their favorite sports for fun, but sometimes they crumble under the pressure of trying to do their best. Mark Twain once referred to golf as a good walk spoiled.

As for intimacy, the eternal attraction and occasional revulsion between men and women means some might fall in and out of love almost as often as Stone Phillips bobs and bounces during a broadcast.

This chapter covers some entertaining and enlightening ideas that will help you neutralize the everyday stress triggers that lurk beneath the surface of relationships. Finessing your stress (rather than obsessing over the inevitable) is a daily practice in self-discipline, open mindedness, wit, and perspective. In building relationships, just as in building physical skills, the more you practice, the better you get. And now, here's this chapter's quiz.

Let's Play Guess Your Stress!

Situation: *You and a friend have made plans for lunch. Your pal is a no show. After thirty minutes of waiting you decide to eat, and by the time you finish an hour has passed. Back at the office you check your calendar. The day and time were correct. You send your friend a quick e-mail expressing regrets that the lunch didn't happen. You get a prompt response stating that the lunch was supposed to be tomorrow, not today. You know that's incorrect because you've had an important meeting scheduled for over a month now, and that meeting is tomorrow.*

You:
1.) Inform your friend in no uncertain terms that it was not you who messed up the date and you have irrefutable proof, should this be necessary.

2.) Decide not to split hairs over who is right or wrong (because you know), and instead ask your friend if there's another date in the near future when the two of you can have lunch.

Debrief: Yes, it's irritating to be stood up, but worse things can happen (muggings, a lost wallet, yellow teeth).

People forget, write down the wrong date or time, or can't always remember commitments they made. Maybe you've made a similar mistake in the past.

It really comes down to whether you want to see your friend and maintain your relationship or write it all off. Having to be right in this situation could cause an unnecessary rift. Would it be worth it?

Maybe your pal is going through a rough period and this is causing forgetfulness and disorganization. Or maybe your friend just isn't as good with a calendar as you. But how you handle this situation could affect what happens between the two of you down the road.

Differences Make a Difference

Ah, relationships! Opposites attract and familiarity breeds contempt—maybe you just can't win. But because so much stress comes from relationships (especially intimate ones), it helps to explore some of the classic gender differences that can cause misunderstandings or conflicts. These differences in perception and communication style don't mean one style is superior to the other, they're simply different.

We hope you'll have fun with this chapter, and that what you read here will help you have more patience with your partner or lover, and others. Maybe you'll be reminded to smile a little more at what makes others tick instead of getting ticked off at them.

Let's start with some of the more obvious differences that exist between men and women.

He Said, She Said

Men don't ever consider calling each other and obsessing over what their spouse or date might have meant when she said what she said. Women never look at another female and wonder, "Could I take her in a fight?"

Men talk in code, agreeing as much on what was not said, as what was. Women don't consider silence an agreement. They want to hear or see confirmation that they're getting through.

Men, when invited somewhere, answer with a "Sure." or "No thanks." And that's the end of the story. Women ask where, when, who with, what's the occasion, and how about the dress code?

Men do not consider going to the bathroom a social opportunity. For them, it's a solo act and for some men, "going" too often is considered a sign of weakness. Women consider a trip to the bathroom as nothing more than an extension of the conversation they're having at the moment, which means they'll go along even if they don't have to "go."

At first it may appear that these gender dissimilarities are just an issue of splitting hairs versus taking things at face value, but you probably agree it's more complicated than that. These few examples are only the tip of the relationship iceberg.

Think of the potential stressing (and blessing) inherent in intimate situations and then brace yourself: there's more. Below are some of our favorite distinctions between how males and females interact with the world and each other, and how stress, the uninvited guest, might crash the party.

Take a Break

Men and women respond differently to malfunctioning or hard-to-operate equipment. When a woman tries to use a tool or piece of machinery, if it doesn't work she says, *Hmmm, I must be doing something wrong!* A man says, *This sucker's broke!*

Lend a Hand

When someone has a problem (whether friend or stranger), women want to offer whatever assistance they can. From making change to mending troubled marriages, women are usually happy to intervene. For the most part, men would prefer not to get involved.

In a public restroom, a woman might declare, *Oh dear, my stall is out of toilet paper!* whereupon she is showered with a multitude of neatly folded wads or streamers from above and below. It is not out of the question that a man might flee the scene rather than invade another fellow's space.

Shop Talk

Women feel their way through a store, getting up close and personal with fabrics, colors, shapes, and textures. They slowly work their way toward the item they are looking for, preferring to take the scenic route through the store. This way, they can enjoy the full experience and maybe stumble onto a surprise item they can't live without.

Like a heat-seeking missile, men focus in on their target. They are there for *one thing only,* and they'll let nothing else slip into the cross hairs. Heading straight toward their destination, they avoid getting too close to merchandise that stands between them and their quarry. They scan the environment, eyes darting from side to side, like both the hunter and the hunted, strategically closing in on the prey.

Just Getting By

Most women are willing to admit they don't know something and are often quick to ask "dumb" questions. They have few qualms about appearing momentarily ignorant.

Men don't like to appear dumb or admit they don't know, so asking for directions or instructions on how to operate something is more difficult for them. Some people joke that the reason Moses wandered through the desert for forty years is because he just couldn't bring himself to stop and ask for directions.

A Question of Expression

In our speeches and training programs, we counsel men never to use one-syllable words when a woman asks, *How do I look in this?* In this situation, a woman desires active engagement, not just lip service. In her mind, syllables denote engagement. The words *nice, good,* or *fine* just don't measure up—and sometimes they are even insulting. *Great* or *svelte* might work in a pinch. But in a woman's mind, generally, the more syllables a man uses, the more points he gets (this assumes positive syllables, of course). We suggest starting out with words like *super* or *lovely,* and working up to *terrific, wonderful, fabulous,* or anything equivalent.

Gender Benders

Women often use more syllables—and words—than men usually want. Men are often looking for a simple yes or no instead of complex sentences, paragraphs, or five-page reports. Men like to keep the word count low, lest they accidentally run out one day. And they get uneasy whenever anyone comes in over budget.

When it comes to expressing needs, there are gender differences, too. A woman will say, *Are you hungry?* when she's the starving one, or *Do you think we should hit this rest stop?* when she's suffering from a bursting bladder and praying for relief. But she forgets that men's bladders go into Standby Mode when they travel, so if the woman doesn't speak up, she's out of luck! When a man does get hungry or needs to stretch his legs, he stops without questions, pronouncements, or fuss.

Most women want their man to share their value about important dates (anniversaries, birthdays, the day they bought the house, got the puppy, etc.). And it's not enough that he remembers, he has to remember for absolutely all the right reasons, or to her, *it's just not the same!*

For some unfathomable reason, however, he is able to retain Super Bowl dates, opening days of hunting season, and when the *Sports Illustrated* swimsuit issue will hit the stands.

Formal, Casual: a Matter of Style

Then there are "style" differences that have nothing to do with gender, but they too are worth fighting over. What's your "time" style, for example? Are you a clock watcher or one who forgets where you're supposed to be, or when?

We ask because there are people who have a *formal* relationship with time *(the time/space continuum and I are joined at the hip...)*, while others have a *casual* relationship with time *(I think I've heard of that time/space continuum thing before...)*.

A Matter of Time

People who have a formal relationship with time don't just show up when they're supposed to—they're always early, just like clockwork. They faithfully wear their watches and check them often. Their operational word is "at," meaning, *I will be there* **at** *2:00*. But they actually show up twenty minutes early, just in case. When travel is involved, they calculate variables such as weather, traffic flow, time of day, construction sites along the route, nearby parking possibilities, number of stairs to climb, or elevator speed.

Whether the venue is work or play, they are reliable to a fault. They take great pride in their promptness and expect similar precision in others. Be advised that you do not want to keep these people waiting (not even one minute), because the formal types keep score. Lateness will be held against you.

People who have a casual relationship with time round off their numbers. Their operational word is "about," meaning *I'll show up* **about** *2:00 or so*. This could mean twenty minutes on either side of the hour, depending on what else is going on. The casual types may range from running a little bit late to showing up on the wrong day, but they take such oversights in stride. Hey, why get upset over an hour or a day? Life being as uncertain as it is, they're just happy they showed up at all and think you should be, too!

As if the issue of time isn't enough to cause worry, anger, or resentment, there are more style differences to consider. You had a hunch, didn't you—we can feel your excitement! Of course, we hope that explaining these conflicting styles will help you be less stressed over them and more open minded once you understand it's nothing personal. It might take a while for you to actually bless these differences, but isn't that a wonderfully optimistic thing to shoot for?

That Thing You Do

You might think that formal and casual time differences would be enough fodder for causing friction in relationships, but because life is filled with adventure and intrigue, there's more. There are people who have a *formal* relationship with things and people who have a *casual* relationship with things.

The formal types are organized and methodical. They are careful with their possessions. Their theme might be, "Neither a borrower nor a lender be." The casual types, unconstrained by standards or systems, are more inclined toward a, "Mi casa es su casa," mindset.

Those who fit in the casual category often typecast the formal beings as rigid and inflexible (actually, anal). The casual ones also think that organized people are just too lazy to look for things. Of course, the formal types get even: they figure the casual ones just ain't playing with a full deck.

Key Notes

The formal types never have to waste time searching for their keys because there's only one spot where such things go. They believe there is only one way for the toilet paper to be positioned on the roller. In fact, a few *extreme* formal types have been known to compulsively flip the toilet paper in other people's bathrooms!

The casual types constantly misplace their keys. Optimists that they are, the keys are never pronounced "lost" because certainly they'll show up, just as they have done in the past. Their cars, handbags, briefcases, or desks are always a mess, but they don't mind searching for things because they're used to it. This is what they do for fun.

As for toilet paper, the casual ones are happy if there is some. Fireworks can ensue when a formal type pairs up with a casual type because the latter doesn't care whether the paper comes off the top or bottom when replacing it. Maybe it would be more correct to say *if* they replace it.

Driving Us Crazy

Formal types are usually fussy about what they drive. When buying a new car they read vehicle reports in magazines and research the internet. They visit dealerships till the sales people know them by name.

They think long and hard about what they want in terms of make, model, color, and interior. And they always choose an option package because standard just isn't good enough.

The casual types aren't even sure what kind of car they drive—after all, there have been so many! Color, make, style, and manufacturer don't fully register with these individuals and that's why they so often lose their cars in parking lots.

If there's more than one vehicle in the family, the casual types might forget which one they're driving on a given day. Being able to punch the alarm button on the remote so their car can identify itself has saved these people hours of roaming and wandering.

To Dine For

Those who are formal with food tend to ritualize everything connected to meals, snacks and drinks. Don't ask them to eat or drink from anything made of plastic or styrofoam. Don't expect them to eat without a napkin. Don't leave the bread wrapper untwisted lest it dry out, or forget to close the cereal box because it might get soggy.

A formal type can buy a monster cookie, break off a little piece, and eat it. They then neatly wrap the cookie back up and stick it in a special spot in a drawer, where they will periodically follow the same routine and snack on the cookie for days.

Those who are extremely casual with food leave boxes open, bottles uncapped, milk cartons on the counter, empty gum wrappers in their handbags or pockets, and they long ago lost the lids to their Tupperware. They use plastic cutlery without complaint and don't care if their crackers are a little soft.

Napkins? Paper towels will do, or maybe even that wadded up tissue that's been knocking around in their handbag or pocket for the last decade. As for the monster cookie, these individuals know that the entire thing must be eaten right now!

Wearing Out

When it comes to clothes, the formal types have a winter wardrobe, a summer wardrobe, a transitional season wardrobe, and specific clothes earmarked for work and play. They may have clothes in their closet that date back to high school, organized and grouped by season, color, and whatever size they happen to be at the time. Obviously, a walk-in closet is a necessity for the formal types, and the only thing better than that is two of them!

The casual types? Well, they have a wardrobe. Sometimes it's easy to find what they want to wear and other times it isn't. Sometimes the clothes fit and sometimes they don't, and that's pretty much it.

Baubles, Bangles, and Beads

The formal types proudly own a few pieces of prized jewelry which they keep sequestered in protective wraps or special containers. The extreme ones store their jewels in a safe deposit box with unrestricted visitation rights. For these individuals, owning jewelry is an important aspect of life; they savor inspecting their collection, stroking and fawning over their favorites.

Casual types often wear jewelry because it seems like a nice idea and helps them fit into the crowd. To these individuals, jewelry is basically the adult equivalent of the fruit loop necklaces and popcorn bracelets of childhood, only the grown-up pieces are more shiny and durable, and you can't eat them.

Paper Chase

Some people have a formal relationship with paper. They are the filers of the world. They like to organize their paper world vertically and keep everything in its assigned space or place, complete with labels or color coding.

Those who have a casual relationship with paper are the pilers. They fill every available horizontal surface with piles of paper, piles of magazines, piles of mail, plus piles of notes, and slips of paper. We call this the hemorrhoid system of paper management. Once in a while these individuals attempt to clear away the piles. They might describe the experience as "feeling like an archeologist," as they sift through ancient documents and notices from events held months ago.

Tool Time

Do a "drive by" along any street in the country, and you'll be able to separate those who have a formal relationship with things from those who have a casual relationship with things. All it takes is a quick glance in the garage.

The formal types have tools, bicycles, and yard equipment hanging neatly on the walls or tidily assembled in a corner. You can tell the casual types because their garages are so crammed with stuff they are forced to park their cars in the driveway.

Play On

Some people have a formal relationship with sports, and others don't. Of course, the formal sports fans can talk endlessly of divisions, teams, players, positions, scores, stats, and recruiting scuttlebutt. You can tell the ones who have a casual relationship with sports because they ask questions like, "Is that the red and yellow team you're talking about?"

True Confessions

You may have already suspected this from earlier comments, but one of your authors (hint: Mimi) has a mostly *formal* relationship with time and things, while your other author (hint: Leslie) has a mostly *casual* relationship with time and things.

For example, Mimi would never go anywhere without at least one timepiece on her person, while Leslie has been known to travel across the country without a watch and not miss it.

Because Mimi has a formal relationship with things, she knows where everything is in her home. While her place doesn't look like that of an obsessive compulsive, she is organized. Leslie once tested Mimi on this issue, asking, *Okay, where are your high school yearbooks?* and in the blink of an eye, Mimi pointed out exactly where they were.

When traveling together, Mimi designates a special place to park her hotel key so she always knows where it is. Leslie, on the other hand, is less methodical. Consequently, she locks herself out of her hotel room at least once per trip.

Perhaps you're wondering if you can be formal with time and casual with things. Yes, you can. This means you'll show up when you're supposed to (or earlier), but you won't have everything you need. If you're lucky, you'll find all the stuff you forgot when you return.

Finesse Your Stress In Style

The point? It doesn't do much good to worry about, get angry or resentful toward, or criticize someone for being different from you. In fact, when it comes to creating a productive workplace or well-functioning family, it's great to have a variety of styles. The formal types can often cover for the casual types and vice versa. Casual types can expose the formal types to "spontaneous adventures" while the formal types can help the casual types remember important dates or commitments.

As you can imagine, nothing is accomplished if one type labels the other as *anal retentive* or if the word *scatter-brained* is bandied about. In short, we are what we are. It's a blessing to learn, grow, change, or modify our own behavior, but when we try to foist our preferences on someone else, it's simply stressing.

After all, if everyone were just like you, would you be necessary? It's nice to be singled out once in a while, or complimented for just being who you are. Knowing that you can't control other people's personalities or behaviors, doesn't it make sense to tolerate these style differences instead of criticizing or judging them? And hey, if we're talking a marriage or long-term relationship, do you suppose some of those obvious differences are what initially attracted you to each other?

Add Some Finesse, Lower Your Stress

Both styles can be influenced from the other's good or bad examples. You already know that rigidity doesn't work (a friendly hint for the formal types), nor does carelessness (casual types, stand up and be counted). This means there's room for adjustment on both sides. Accepting and adapting the best of the best from each style is in itself an exercise in finesse.

Okay, so you have these little differences to cope with, and you are probably willing to admit they're not really all that tough to tolerate, when you put your mind to it. But style differences aside, in the bigger scheme of things, you actually have a lot in common with the rest of your species.

For example, health and happiness, security and peace of mind are what most of us desire. But the collective stress we all appear to share, that commonplace floating anxiety that seems in endless supply—is one bond we all might be better off without.

Give Us this Day Our Daily Dread

Think of the social pressures that can keep you stressed if you fall prey to their influence—the urgent, insistent messages that keep so many hurrying, worrying, and scurrying like the whimpering rabbit from *Alice in Wonderland.* Newspaper headlines flaunt the *disaster du jour,* while the nightly news parades images of war, political unrest, terror, homicide, and other forms of human suffering sandwiched between streams of witless commercials.

Many of the ads are for prescription drugs, something you may feel a need for, now that your brain has been bombarded with all this bad news! But the last story is always a brief piece designed to make you smile or feel warm inside, regardless of the grim fare that preceded it. Once the worrisome reports are gone, you're given a lineup of the network's shows for the evening. The agenda has subtly shifted back to entertainment.

But a lot of what you saw and heard isn't always easy to forget. You might find yourself wondering if you and your family will be safe, if you might be a candidate for an antidepressant, or if your pet is feeling secretly resentful about its current brand of food.

Worry Happens

Here we are, citizens in a Nation O' Plenty, riled and worried about cholesterol, wrinkles, age spots, road rage, the stock market, and unsightly dandruff, to name a few. But what good is worry, really? It only causes you to fret or stew. It encourages your inner brat to project a mental film festival of worst case scenarios.

The horrors you imagine will either happen or they won't (research suggests that most of what we worry about never happens). *But because worry is negative fixation on a future state of being, it corrodes your present.* How can you be fully in the moment when you're so fixed on unknown disasters that might overtake you in the next hour or two, tomorrow, or even a year from now?

Anger Occurs

Anger, while an "in the moment" emotion, can sometimes be a catalyst for change, but anger turns self-defeating when it becomes a habit. Too many people are the victims of unrelieved anger, and all that stored up negative energy has the potential for triggering uncontrolled outbursts. That's what happened in the nineties when the word rage became so commonplace.

People lost their tempers over trivial incidents, and some of them paid dearly for their out-of-control moment. We're not suggesting you should never get angry or that you should stifle it. We're saying that in many instances, when your mind is turned toward blessing instead of stressing, anger doesn't even have to enter the picture.

After a seminar, one of our participants came up to us, complaining about a woman who applied a coat of nail polish during our session (we hadn't noticed). She declared, "I was so angry over her rudeness I wasn't able to hear what either of you were saying!" Here's a good question to ask in situations like this: *Who owns this problem?*

Our poor victim gladly took on someone else's problem, and she was the worse for it. She couldn't distinguish between acceptance and approval. She didn't know about accepting the uncontrollables or letting go of useless anger, but you do. Why obsess over something you're not in charge of? That's what finessing your stress is all about.

Resentment Roils

Resentment is what happens when anger remains un-resolved—when anger of the moment collects, grows into a massive hairball, and begins to fester. When we are unwilling (or perhaps unable) to resolve an issue; when we can't forgive, forget, or come to terms with an unfortunate inci-dent, resentment intensifies. Actually, it metastasizes, and you are the only person negatively affected by it.

Some people hold onto their resentment for years, as if it were an emotional IRA plan, accumulating compound interest and someday could be cashed in for big bucks. Why would you want to give away your personal power and peace of mind over something as worthless as resentment?

Removing the W.A.R.T.

Here's the nutshell version: Worry + Anger + Resent-ment = Tension. We call this the W.A.R.T. equation. Who, other than a toad, would want to grow such an unsightly thing? Well, you have a lot more going for you than any amphibian. You possess a secret remedy that can make the W.A.R.T. go missing if you choose to use it. Tada!

Enter the miracle product, W.A.R.T. Begone. Simply put, this wonderful application is all about your ability to ratio-nally separate a Triggering event from your External response. It's your willingness and ability to **T.I.E.** one on.

Your Internal response, your ability to consciously de-cide how you will interpret and respond to a situation, is your personal miracle cure. When you keep yourself fully present and in the moment, you can sidestep the far too common reactions of anger, worry, and resentment. Instead, you can face stressful situations in a rational frame of mind.

You have the essential ingredients to produce a lifetime supply of W.A.R.T. Begone. Think of this wonderful product as a personal, fast-acting, long-lasting agent guaranteed to keep your outlook light and your spirit buoyant. You no longer have to let unnecessary worry, anger, or resentment undermine your outlook.

The Present of Presence

Hey, why let the little things corrupt your existence? Why let little irritations interfere with your important relationships? Why let personal styles or innate differences get in the way of your (or a loved one's) happiness? Life is too short to let the annoyances take over!

Finessing your stress means being mentally alert and fully present to whatever is going on around you. From now on, when potential stressors rise out of the mist, mindfully summon your inner resources so you can be fully present to what's going on.

Frequent applications of W.A.R.T. Begone makes it far easier for you to shake off past or future stressing so you can catch all the blessings that are right in front of you. Who could ask for anything more?

Chapter 8
Press Your Stress

RUBES®

By Leigh Rubin

138

Chapter 8
Press Your Stress

Happiness? That's nothing more than health and a poor memory.
—Albert Schweitzer

Trying To Have It Both Ways

Maybe you, like so many others, enjoy "people watching" when you get the chance, and you'd have to admit, people are quite a study. Just eavesdrop on someone else's conversation for a few minutes, and you get some quick insights about human behavior—the good, the bad, and the ugly.

Funny, it's relatively easy to pinpoint the contradictions between what others say they want and what they actually do, but it's not such a breeze to catch ourselves. Human nature abounds with paradox. Consider that there are leagues of people who:

O *Want to be thin, but eat too much*
O *Want to be healthy, but don't get enough exercise*
O *Want to be happy, but their attitudes leave a lot to be desired*
O *Want to be better parents, but don't educate themselves on how to improve*
O *Want to be unique, but feel self-conscious when they don't fit in*
O *Want to be rich, but squander their money and keep themselves in debt*
O *Want more free time, but fill what little leisure time they have with obligations and trivial tasks*
O *Want to feel less stressed, but choose behaviors that increase anxiety and tension*

O   Want to have inner peace and solitude, but surround themselves with noise and distraction
O   Want to have a good intimate relationship, but aren't willing to do the work
O   Want to feel more relaxed, but can't sit down long enough to let it happen

Given these discrepancies, it's obvious that we have our work cut out for us. Maybe we could just chalk it up to the human condition and admit we all have a natural talent for complicating our own lives. But it doesn't mean the situation is hopeless. It just takes commitment and a willingness to firm up your mind, body, and spirit.

As you read this book, maybe it seems like you're involved in a *mental* fitness program, and that's correct. While many people are faithful about training their bodies, few put their brains through any kind of conditioning program.

A Perfect Fit

Chapters four through six focus on the mental aspects of blessing your stress, and we hope you'll review this section often. We also hope the key ideas from those chapters (word use, unsinkable self-talk, giving the inner brat a time out) are making a difference for you. These key skills can help you every day of your life if you're willing to practice them. Just like the benefits of exercising regularly, the potential is enormous.

In the world of pumping iron, they often say, "No pain, no gain," but we're not so sure about that. When it comes to personal change, we endorse a kinder, gentler approach: no strain, no gain. After all, you don't want you to hurt yourself and drop out of the program! But if you choose the strain—and gain—of discipline, you avoid the pain of regret. In this chapter you'll find a variety of ideas for keeping both your mind and body fit. But first, a warm up: here's the quiz.

Let's Play Guess Your Stress!

Situation: *One of your favorite stores is going out of business and they've discounted all their merchandise. Each week the discounts have gotten deeper, but there's no guarantee that the jacket you've been lusting over will still be available the last day of the sale. You either risk paying a little bit more or you risk not getting the item at all. The store will only be open four more days and the coveted jacket is still on the shelves. By the end of the week, it will be 60% off instead of the 40% discount on the sticker today.*

You:
1.) Wait till no one is looking and tuck the jacket behind the boxes stacked under some shelves. This way, by Thursday or Friday no one will have bought it and you'll not only end up with what you want, you'll get the best price, too.

2.) You take the item to the counter and buy it before anyone else nabs it. You get a good deal, the store makes a few bucks as they prepare to close their doors, and everyone ends up getting something. In fact, you wear your new jacket out of the store, you like it so much.

Debrief: Getting a good deal seems to be the great American pastime, but in this situation, there are ethical issues to consider. At the risk of sounding uppity, would your jacket look and feel as good if you cheated on the purchase, or would it not make a difference? Buying it now means you don't have to worry about the possibility of getting caught in an act of deception by people who have enjoyed you as a customer. Nor would you have any chafing flashbacks whenever you put the jacket on or run into anyone who worked at the store. Buy it now, and you can wear it with a clear conscience.

It's a Fine, Fine Line

Studies over the last two decades reveal that people are less conscientious about ethics than they once were. It appears that many individuals are more tolerant of—if not more disposed toward—office theft, cheating on exams, falsifying work experience, switching price tags, and other ways of behaving badly.

Then there's the lengthy list of famous mugs you've seen on TV: corporate executives whose ethical practices are so riddled with stretch marks that cosmetic surgery wouldn't even help. Some have escaped censure, while others have had to publicly pay for their sins. In her temporary fall from grace, Martha Stewart's ankle bracelet wasn't exactly a fashion statement. But high profile or not, getting caught trying to sneak across that fine deception line can be stressful indeed, and who needs that kind of hassle?

Another Fine Distinction

Oops, we did it! We dared mention the word *deception*, and there's a wee bit of it going on in our society today. The overstatements in commercials are enough to make you laugh out loud. Just how excited can someone really get over a shampoo, electric shaver, or household cleanser; and why do advertisers use models who aren't old enough to vote in wrinkle cream ads?

You've no doubt noticed the popularity of prescription drug ads on TV. They're thicker than mosquitoes in the

Okeefenokee Swamp! Nowadays, drug companies want *you* to tell *your* doctor *you* need medication! Funny, it used to be the other way around.

Consider the suggestive ad for GAD: Generalized Anxiety Disorder. The name is vague, but it sounds so ominous. Note the indefinite language (hint: the word *generalized*) and the misleading nature of the subtext. *Uh oh, you could have it and not even know!* If you don't know you have it, then why would you need to be treated for it?

The GAD thing may not end here. There's too much potential for escalation. Consider GADS: Generalized Anxiety Disorder Syndrome, because a simple GAD condition isn't bad enough. Or how about EGADS : Extreme Generalized Anxiety Disorder? Every time you add a word, the condition worsens. YEGADS! Reach for a chill pill! Or is that something you have to get from your doctor, too?

A Lost Art
Speaking of magic pills, a dermatologist recently told us it's hard treating skin disorders these days because patients are too impatient. They don't want to wait and give the medicine time to work—they want an instant cure.

What else would you expect, really? We live in a "now" culture with access to instant downloads, instant replays, instant purchases, instant meals, instant photos, instant videos, instant money, instant access to hundreds of TV channels, and more.

People are restless and impatient, sighing and tapping their feet while waiting for the computer to boot up, the printer or copier to do its thing, the web site to load, the microwave to ding. Sound like anyone you know? Patience is a lost art. With everyone so busy, who has time for it?

But, just like a Broadway revival of *42nd Street* or *South Pacific*, we'd like to bring that old classic, patience, and introduce it to a new audience. We're hoping for a long run, and would like to see you there, front row, center.

The Fine Art of Wait Lifting

John Lennon said "Life is what happens while you're making other plans," and life seems to be happening faster and faster each year. Society's accelerated pace has wildly distorted everyone's perceptions of time, and that's one of the reasons people are so impatient.

Our inner clocks have been revved up to the point that the passing of a few seconds feels like minutes, and minutes feel like hours. Chronic impatience has reached the point where some people feel they "don't have time to be polite." Give us a break! Just how long does it take to say hello, please, or thank you?

Technology plays a major role in today's time bind. Technology has made life so convenient, people have lost their tolerance for inconvenience. Instant access to so much information, stimulation, and recreation spoils us and foils what little patience we have left. But there's a cure for this condition. Enter the fine art of Wait Lifting, an essential skill for the 21st century.

To get your head around how convenient and time efficient your life actually is (even though it doesn't feel that way), think for a moment about the millions of people in this world who are living in makeshift shelters, plowing fields with oxen, washing clothes by hand, cooking over an open fire, and walking several miles for food, medicine, and even emergency medical treatment.

Walking, for God's sake! Not for exercise, but because that's their only mode of transportation, regardless of the weather. Too bad there isn't a Third World Network we can tune into when we start feeling discontented with our lot. The images would remind us how truly blessed we are.

If you've joined the ranks of the rushed, the mushed, the pressed, the stressed, we'd like to help reacquaint you with an old friend. Your long lost patience, once resurrected, will help you handle the waits of the world.

Just as you slowly increase your exercise intensity when getting more fit, we suggest you do the same for your wait lifting program. Start with light waits first, then when you're ready, move to medium waits. Save the heavy waits for later.

Wait a Minute

Light waits include patiently hanging out while the toaster or coffee maker do their thing. From there, let your computer or printer warm up without any tsks or sighs. If you're still on dial up, allow web sites to load without cursing or banging your head against the desk. Let the frozen dinners cook in the microwave without intervention (it's programmed—it knows what it's doing).

Traffic lights belong in the light wait category (though it may not feel like it if you're in a massive rush), and so do most answering machine messages (don't hang up!). *Mind you, we're talking seconds and minutes here, not glacial time.* Work on this idea so you can put these things in perspective.

Once you've mastered the light waits, you can move on in your training program.

As you advance to medium waits, you're ready to take on slow trains, sluggish elevators, or bide your time at the doctor's office. From there, try finding a parking place near the mall entrance without tooth grinding or hair pulling, standing in supermarket lines without ripping open the bag of chips, dealing with doltish drivers without pounding your dashboard, and not calling to check on your takeout order when delivery takes a few minutes longer than usual.

Get Your Wait Under Control

And finally, when you're bulked up enough to deal with heavy waits, you can tackle serious traffic back ups, delayed and canceled flights, the interminable time lapse between having a medical procedure and getting the report, saving money for a special purchase rather than relying on credit, and waiting for your kids to grow up. Heavy wait lifting also involves having the strength to quit putting off the important things, to "do it now," while you still can.

To demonstrate how far you've come in your wait lifting program, take time to call or hand write a note to someone you miss. Take extra moments to hug your loved ones, to listen to them with both ears, or to tell them how much they mean to you. Carve out a few minutes for more exercise and healthier eating.

And last, take on the big things: quit smoking, take that dream vacation you've been putting off for too long, mend that troubled relationship, or get out of a bad one before it's too late.

Last Call

If you were lying on your deathbed right now (God forbid), what unfinished business would there be? What would you be wishing you had done? Lift the wait from your shoulders and go do it now; make it happen. Don't put the important things off too long or the opportunity may pass you by. To help you work on your wait lifting skills, it's time to open your Bless Your Stress journal and make some notes.

How would you describe the extent of your patience (or impatience) level?

O *I'm one of the most patient people I know because...*

O *I'm okay most of the time except for...*

O *I could use a few wait lifting sessions because...*

O *I need some intensive wait training—and I need it now because...*

O *The circumstances in which I am most patient involve...*

O *I tend to be my most impatient when...*

O *I could help myself build up my wait lifting skills if I were to...*

Lighten the Wait

Wait lifting sessions are a good time to review what's right in your life, and we have something that can help. We have a little card you can carry with you. It's a Gratitude List card, and it takes very little time to fill it out: just write down the five things in life most important to you and then tuck the card in your wallet.

Whenever you start getting impatient or stressed over stuff that really doesn't matter, pull out the card and read it. You'll get *instant* perspective. If you'd like an official version of the card instead of making your own, send a self-addressed, stamped envelope to: Gratitude Card, Box 956, East Lansing, MI 48826.) We'll be happy to send you one.

Mind Your Mind, Mind Your Body

Throughout this book we illustrate how you can make the shift from stressing to blessing by retooling your thought patterns, and we've tried to do it in an imaginative way. You now know that by combining self-discipline and creativity you can permanently transform your perspective and get more out of life. Yes, you *can* retrain your brain. But (and you probably expected this) there's more.

Your brain may now be buff, but then there's your body to consider. Forgive the boldness, but if you were back in school taking a health class and your teacher assigned a grade based on the overall condition of your physical self, would you get a Pass, Fail, or Incomplete?

Worth Noting

You know that your brain listens to everything you say when you talk to yourself. Are you listening when your body talks to you? Every symptom you experience—tension or anxiety, pain or discomfort, stomach or sleep problems, and so on—is your body's way of communicating with you.

Think of stress symptoms as "postcards" from your body. Read these messages, and like a conscientious correspondent, respond in a timely fashion. Don't let those post-cards get forwarded to the dead letter office!

Some people act as if they've developed an allergy to exercise. They say they're not the exercise type, or they don't have time for it. Or they don't like to sweat. Maybe they're in the same camp as Joan Rivers, who once said, "I don't work out. If God had wanted us to bend over, He would have put diamonds on the floor."

Well, here's some good news about exercise—it doesn't have to be done at world class level. Your buns don't have to turn into steel, but wouldn't you like them to have a consistency firmer than bread dough? It's recently been discovered that exercise is cumulative; you don't have to do it all at once. You can enhance your physical fitness by simply moving more! Try walking, for example. A bunch of extra steps and short walks can add up by the end of the day. Think J.D.S.—Just Do Something!

Stepping Out

Get in the habit of routinely parking your car a little farther from your destination. If you're in decent shape and wouldn't need a resuscitation team at the end of your trip, take a flight of stairs or two instead of the elevator. If you're shopping at the mall, walk from one end to the other just for the heck of it.

Stretch more, too. There are exercise classes everywhere today—gyms, clubs, wellness centers, community ed. You can sign up for martial arts, kick boxing, Pilates, ballet, tap, Nia dancing, jazz, ballroom, belly dancing, clogging, hip hop, and other fun forms of movement. Or just put on your favorite music and free dance when no one is looking.

Go wild or mild, but at least do a little something every day.

There was a time when, if you were overweight and out of shape and wanted to get more fit, you had to endure the humiliation of walking into a gym filled with a bevy of bouncing busybodies sweating in skimpy spandex suits. But for women, there's now the option called Curves. It's a friendly, gentle approach to body conditioning for women of all ages, sizes, and levels of experience in exercising.

The Key Three

Body maintenance involves three key components: strength, endurance, and flexibility. *Strength* is built through weight training or resistance exercises (sit ups, push ups, leg lifts, for example). You won't necessarily turn into *The Terminator* or *Cat Woman,* but you'll increase your muscle mass and that's a good thing, especially if you're over forty.

Endurance is the cardio component. Your heart is a muscle, and you can keep your ticker in top shape by fast walking, swimming, biking, jogging, and so on. The jogging craze that began thirty years ago taught us the benefits of building our endurance and cardio capacity.

You don't have to turn into a marathoner, but you can gain a lot of benefits by simply walking briskly. This is good news for those who think running is an unnatural act, unless they're dashing to a bathroom or trying to avoid someone.

Flexibility rounds out the triad and is perhaps the most neglected. Even some professional athletes don't include flexibility as part of their fitness regimen, but daily stretching will help you maintain or even increase your range of motion.

Sure, maybe you can run three miles but what's with those velcro shoe closures? If it's hard reaching your shoe laces, stretching can help. This way, as you get older you won't need one of those shoehorns with the handle that almost reaches to your waist. Check out the books, classes, or videos on stretching, yoga, Tai Chi, and more.

Move On

It's important to find the kind of exercise you enjoy so you'll stay with it for the long term. If you're the type who needs to make a commitment, sign up for a class. If you're an independent learner, buy a video and exercise at your convenience. For most people, walking is an easy, convenient, low investment exercise (a pair of good shoes is the only requirement).

You just need to know your exercise preferences so you can create a workout routine you'll keep for life. And you've heard this one before—if you have never done anything more strenuous than brushing your teeth or clipping nose hairs, check with your doctor first.

Exercising should be something you look forward to and appreciate. Don't try to conform to what someone else thinks you should do. Every person is different. For example, one of your authors (hint: Mimi) belongs to a gym where she uses the weight equipment and participates in aerobic dance classes three times a week and spinning when the mood strikes. Because she lives in LA, sometimes she gets to work out with celebrities!

Your other author (hint: Leslie) exercises in her home with yoga and Pilates tapes, a treadmill and free weights so she can stay in shape for riding her horse and playing disc golf. Neither would be enthralled with the other's workout programs, but the point is that both are regular exercisers, committed to activities they find enjoyable and helpful.

Take a Seat Now and Then, Too

We've just covered the importance of movement and exercise, now let's talk about the opposite. Remember that stuff about *sitting still* covered earlier in the book? You probably know how hard it can be to just sit and try to relax and not do anything else. But in a book about stress, we'd be remiss if we didn't bring up the practice of meditation.

Our intent is not to teach you about meditation but we encourage you to investigate what it is and how it might help you. Many people mistakenly think that meditation means making the mind a total blank, and because they can't achieve this, they figure they're doing it "wrong" and they give up.

Jakuso Kwong sums up the meditation process nicely: "Don't chase after thoughts and don't push them away. Just let them come in and go out like a swinging door."

In addition to helping individuals relax, heal their spirits, find inner peace, and seek their spiritual path, meditation is now used by health practitioners in cardiac rehab, pain management, anxiety reduction, and more. There are several types of meditation, and you can find out more by reading a few books or signing up for a class. It's definitely worth checking out.

Multi Me

And now, do a quick seat belt check. We're taking a sharp turn to the other side of the spectrum: from doing nothing to doing too much. It's called multitasking and it's a national sport. Whether the venue is home or the work-place, there seems to exist an irresistible gravitational pull toward multitasking.

We human beings suddenly morph into *human doings* as we try our hardest to do our jobs, handle interruptions, meet the demands of urgent and important tasks, complete our routine chores, fulfill our many personal and profes-sional obligations, handle shifting priorities, and cope with unanticipated circumstances. Whew!

Odd, isn't it. Machines and electronics were supposed to simplify life, make things easier, and give us back more time. Instead, the opposite has happened—our days are in-creasingly more busy, more demanding, and more complex. It almost seems, that in some ways, technology has enslaved, rather than saved us.

For years now, the organizational mantra has been "do more with less" and if you're like everyone else, you've taken this message to heart in both your work and personal life. You're doing more, moving faster, working longer hours, coping with ever expanding to-do lists, trying to balance the demands and obligations of multiple roles, while hop-ing to have some kind of life at the end of the day. What's wrong with this picture?

TV is a notorious multitasker. Witness the crawl, flashes of upcoming shows, weather bulletins, school closings, breaking news, sports scores, stock reports, and more. But it's the computer that reigns as our primary multitasking guru. And because computers can do it so well, the rest of us think we can, too, if we just try hard enough. Hullo!

But you aren't a machine and you aren't programmed with Windows! Your mind can't efficiently and effectively split its operations like software can. Yeah we know, we can hear you protest.

You're a better multitasker than everyone you know, right? You started multitasking long before it was fashionable. You've perfected your system. So eat that sandwich, grab that remote, call a friend, and make a note as you read on.

Me, Myself and I

Multitasking feels good because it gives the illusion of productivity. It also fractures your focus and increases the possibility of errors. Multitasking can increase your stress because it occurs in a flurry of activity, motion, and random mental energy. It's the opposite of concentration.

Multitasking deludes you into thinking you're being efficient but take a moment and think of the mistakes you make when you try to do too many things at once. Would you want a surgeon to multitask while working on you?

Yet multitasking is embedded in our culture, more the norm than the exception. How long has it been since you sat and ate a meal without reading or watching TV? Think of the multitasking you do when driving. And don't you wonder when you pass someone who is driving, smoking, and talking on their cell at the same time—or worse—reading at the wheel?

You probably realize that splitting your focus and occupying yourself with multiple tasks can lead to mistakes, errors in judgment, and sometimes even accidents. You've seen countless yahoos yammering on their cells, endangering themselves and others, doing a lousy job of parking, merging, or changing lanes.

The point, of course, is that multitasking is an excuse to rush, listen poorly, or do such a sloppy job that it will have to be done all over again. In the long run, where is that going to get you? Let others be the bad example of the multitasking fallacy rather than you.

You can now burn a calorie or two by reaching for your Bless Your Stress journal and cataloguing how exercise, re-laxation, and multitasking fit in your life.

About exercise (choose the one that best describes you):

O   *I already exercise on a regular basis.*

O   *I think about exercising on a regular basis.*

O   *I know I need to start exercising on a regular basis.*

About relaxation and quiet time (again, choose the one that best describes you):

O   *I make it a daily practice to spend some time sitting still and being quiet.*

O   *I am pretty good about taking a few moments now and then, to sit quietly and relax.*

O   *I would rather have an invasive medical procedure than be asked to sit still and do nothing.*

About multitasking (you know the drill):

O   I gave up multitasking a long time ago.

O   I am extremely selective about multitasking because I understand its drawbacks.

O   I can't give up my multitasking. You wouldn't believe how much I've gotten done while reading this chapter!

To help you make a commitment (or stay committed) to a more balanced, less frenetic daily regimen, briefly complete these sentences:

O   I can carve out more time for a regular exercise plan if I...

O   The exercise that would be best for me is...

O   I can spend a few quiet "do nothing" minutes a day if I...

O   I can better monitor my tendency to multitask if I were to...

No More Bad Breath

When the long lived actress, Sophie Tucker, was asked about the secret to longevity, her answer was, "Keep breathing!" When Dr. Andrew Weil, the health guru, was asked if there were one single thing a person could do to enhance overall health and well-being, his answer was, "Breathing."

Well, there's breathing, and then there's breathing, but who consciously thinks about this life-giving, autonomic function? This may sound bizarre, but there are all kinds of breathing disciplines and practices. Just pop the word into a search engine sometime when you're online and you will discover vast and varied approaches to what would seem a mundane, ho hum subject.

Right now, shift your attention to your breath. Are you breathing from your chest or your belly? Are your breaths shallow or deep? Most of us have no clue about our breathing patterns, but here are some points to remember. When you're stressed, you will have a tendency to hold your breath or breathe in short, shallow gasps through your mouth. This will increase your anxiety.

Your breath should come from your belly, not your chest. Breathe in and out through your nose, not your mouth. Expand your belly on the inhale and gently contract your stomach muscles on the exhale. Teach yourself to make periodic breath checks throughout the day so you can become more aware of your breathing patterns. Whenever you start feeling stressed, stop. Take a deep breath (through your nose). Slowly inhale, then slowly exhale. Remain still, and repeat this cycle three times.

You can't be both stressed and blessed at the same time: taking deep, slow breaths will help calm and center you. It will help you relax and regroup so you can think more clearly. Some people put a little sign in their office that simply says "BREATHE" so they can remember to take a nice deep breath every now and then.

The Food Chain

Now that you've considered what you do *with* your body, it's time to contemplate what you put *in* it. You can be foolish or "fuelish" about food. Start thinking of good food (that is, healthy food) as a clean burning high-octane fuel which will give you less gas and better mileage. Anyone with more self-awareness than an iguana knows there's a difference between *brain* hunger and *stomach* hunger, and that it's a bad idea to "feed" anger or loneliness.

The illuminating book, *Diets Don't Work*, suggests that you eat only when you're hungry and quit when you're full because whatever calories you don't burn off in a day will get stored as fat. What a blinding flash of the obvious!

Serving Suggestions

1) *The drink link.* Sometimes people think they're hungry when they are actually thirsty. Drink more water throughout the day, and fewer soft drinks or coffee, to regulate your appetite and keep your body in balance. If you don't like the taste of water, try adding some lemon. Water, like breathing, is vital to your health.

2) *In praise of the graze.* Miss Piggy advises that you should never eat more than you can lift. Eat several small meals a day instead of three big ones. Snack on a piece of fruit and nuts or cheese instead of sweets. Eat fruits and vegetables in their natural state—an apple rather than applesauce, for example. Break with tradition and make your dinner the lightest meal of the day so you don't go to bed stuffed.

3) *Be a neater eater.* Some people practically have to be hosed down after a meal! You can add to your eating pleasure by slowing down. Don't inhale your food, but inhale its aromas before you start eating. Cut a small piece and chew each bite thoroughly before swallowing.

Put your knife and fork down while you're chewing. Empty your mouth before you refill your fork. Common sense, yes, but look around the next time you're in a restaurant and see how few people actually do this.

4) *Fall back on a snack.* If you are eating a snack food (popcorn, chips, pretzels, etc.), contrary to the commercials, we bet you can eat, chew, and swallow one at a time! Whether snack or meal, when you eat, serve yourself smaller portions and eat more slowly. This gives your brain a better chance to signal when you are getting full.

5) *Combat the fat.* When you fry or saute` use a nonstick spray. If you need an oil, use olive or canola. Try a little broth, juice, or wine, too. When baking, use two egg whites rather than one whole egg (who will know?). Don't eat chicken skin; that's where the fat is. And yes, that's why it tastes so good. Remove skin and visible fat from meat before cooking.

As for the obvious: avoid fried foods and cut down on your salt (oops, so much for french fries!). Rather than using loads of salad dressing, lightly dip your fork into it before you take a bite of salad. You'll use significantly less.

6) *If you're able, read the label.* If you can't pronounce it, maybe you shouldn't eat it. The word hydrogenated means a normally unsaturated fat was made saturated (bad fat!) by adding extra hydrogen atoms (a liquid turned into a solid). This is not good. Crackers, cookies, cake mixes, and snack items are the most notorious, but now you can buy trans fat-free versions of some (this is good). Many imitation dairy products contain coconut or palm oil, the only saturated fat that comes from a vegetable source (this is not so good).

7) *Hedge the edge.* If you're ravenous, drink a glass of water or eat half an apple before a meal to take the edge off. A small glass of milk or juice might also work.

8) *Don't bloat; make a note.* When you have a moment, write down the foods that make you feel full and bloated. List the wholesome foods and snacks you could substitute for the heavy, fat-laden ones. Put the really unhealthy foods (you know what they are) on the occasional list instead of the everyday one. When you're dining out with a friend or loved one, consider sharing an entree. Who knows, with these strategies, you might end up feeling better and even losing a few pounds, too.

9) *Is it worth the extra girth?* Don't completely cut out your favorites, just cut down the amounts. Don't slather butter or margarine on toast, bread, pancakes, etc., as if you were applying sunscreen to your body. Eliminate butter on sandwiches; cut down on mayonnaise. Stressed is "desserts" spelled backwards; if you're going to indulge, do it at lunch and this way, you'll have a chance to work it off. Or just take a few slow, scrumptious bites—and leave the rest. Yeah, we know *exactly* how hard this is! But this way you won't have to feel so deprived.

10) *Enlist the fist.* Make a loose fist and study it for a moment. That's the approximate size of your stomach. Before you eat a meal, look at your fist as a reminder of your stomach's true capacity. The point is to make your hunger go away but that doesn't mean you have to eat everything. You can waste food or waist food—get over that old childhood programming about having to clean your plate. As Ziggy once said, "The waist is a terrible thing to mind."

Eat, Drink, and Be Merry, for Tomorrow We May Diet

Eating healthier doesn't mean a subsistence diet of roots and berries for the rest of your life nor does it mean you'll never have fun at the table again. Think of the word diet as a noun rather than a verb (a diet is for life, while *dieting* means denial and strife). Moderation is the key. You might be shocked and maybe a little embarrassed to discover how little food your body really needs. We were.

These tips have been brought to you by two "foodies" who would rather live to eat than eat to live. We can both bear witness to how well these principles work, regardless of how grudgingly we embraced them in the beginning. And we also will be quick to confess that we, like everyone else (except perhaps Drs. Ornish and Perricone), have our lapses. We try to enjoy our momentary indulgences because they don't happen all that often anymore.

And now, some quick notes for your Bless Your Stress journal:

O   *Given these tips on trying more healthful eating, one thing I need to do right away is...*

O   *I can cut down out some of the fat in my diet if I...*

O   *One way I can persuade myself to eat more fiber is...*

O   *I can encourage myself to drink more water if I...*

O   *One attitude shift I need to make about eating is...*

Pressing On

You've been hit with a lot of dos and don'ts in this chapter, but that's what pressing your stress is all about. It isn't that you don't know many of these things, but maybe you haven't pushed yourself to the point where you admit, accept, and apply what you know.

Just as a stuck car sometimes needs to "rock 'n roll" to get free, you might want to give yourself a friendly shove, or spend some quality time with your iProd so you can make the commitment and move on.

You probably know people who whimper, wail, and wring their hands over what's wrong in their lives, but that's the only course of action they take. They're the ones with the bumper sticker that reads, "Exercise daily. Eat wisely. Die anyway."

Rather than taking the next steps or looking for what's right in their lives, they stay stuck in one spot. Sitting in the middle of their rat-infested island of self-imposed woes, they turn themselves into mental castaways, held captive by their own misery. But you know better. You're willing to press your stress because of the rewards on the other side, better health and more happiness.

A Peace of the Whole

Life is precious. You are in charge of your stress and health for your entire lifetime. Yes, you will need the services of a physician or alternative health practitioner (or both), but ultimately, you are in charge of your well-being.

The purpose of this book is to highlight the idea that you are filled with untapped potential—that your mind and body share a mystical connection that deserves exploration and cultivation. But it's not enough to think or talk about these ideas. As the Chinese proverb reminds us, "Talk does not cook rice."

Each day you have an opportunity to enhance the whole of who you are, mentally, physically, and spiritually. Much of *Bless Your Stress* emphasizes what it takes to make the most of your mind because that's where it all begins. In this frantic, time-deprived, distracting culture of ours, it's hard settling into yourself.

But when you're in a place of inner peace and self-acceptance you become more comfortable with who you are. You feel more confident. When you start controlling the things you can (your words, your perspective, your choices), you can't help but grow spiritually. But your body needs proper care and nourishment too, and now you know what it takes to keep your whole self in tune.

When you are patient enough to consciously and carefully nurture the unique and magical balance of your mind-body connection, it's guaranteed you'll feel blessed indeed.

Chapter 9
Bless Your Stress

A blessing in disguise

Chapter 9
Bless Your Stress

The way I see it, if you want the rainbow
you've gotta put up with the rain.
—Dolly Parton

Blessings in Disguise

Ask your friends to list the things in life they don't want to have happen and their list would likely include losing a loved one, getting fired, going through a divorce, and having an accident or major health incident. We all know that life is filled with hills and valleys, but it's a lot more comfortable sitting on the hill and watching someone else trudge their way out of the valley than making the climb yourself. For treks of this nature, you have to carry your own weight. No Sherpas allowed.

In the scheme of life, hills and valleys make up a whole, like pancakes and syrup, chips and salsa. Maybe you've read some biographies of famous or successful people: stories filled with challenge, despair, determination, and eventual triumph. They stand as examples of how adversity and opportunity are opposite ends of the same thread.

Take divorce for example. It's a painful, difficult process, but in time it can also be liberating, empowering, and filled with self-discovery. For some, losing a job marks the end of the road, while for others, it represents the chance to start a business and fulfill a life dream.

The Best of Times, the Worst of Times

The worst of times are first cousin to the best of times.

Bad things happen, and as hard as it is to believe, even the toughest times can bring some small blessings. For instance, an outpouring of empathy and support can help heal an aching heart and fill some empty spaces left by loss. What initially feels like a bad experience can sometimes yield positive outcomes.

For example, ending a dysfunctional relationship can open a door to new possibilities. Talk with someone who has experienced divorce and you may hear a similar tale. Then there's our friend Mike McKinley, who survived with cancer in his late thirties. Mike says, "It was the best thing that ever happened to me because that's when I really started living."

The tough times, not the easy ones, teach us life's richest lessons. This is because pain and raw hurt open up a window through which you view the world in a way you never have before. During this period, you're more sensitive, tuned in, and receptive to learning. As you heal, the vista begins to fade, but if you hold onto the insights, you gain in wisdom and depth of character.

Yet in a world filled with so much convenience and emphasis on lifestyle (rather than life itself), it's tempting to push the panic button and treat minor incidents like 911 calls. Is it really a sign of Armageddon that you can't find the mate to the only pair of shoes that matches your new suit, or that the bank's computer is down and the transaction must be done by hand?

Unfathomable as it may seem, people used to do all kinds of transactions by hand—back in the Stone Age a few decades ago. And no one felt inconvenienced. Every now and then you just have to get a grip, and keep life's awful inevitables in perspective. This way, you can stockpile those sighs and tsks for the times you really need them. Speaking of inescapable inconveniences, let's go on to the quiz.

Let's Play Guess Your Stress!

Situation: *You haven't made many purchases on the Internet, and you're still a bit leery about it. But you've found an item on ebay that is too good to pass up. As a newbie to the wonders of this vast virtual swap meet, you diligently jump through the hoops, putting in the required information one uncertain step at a time. With your cursor poised to hit the "bid now" button, the screen goes black. A power failure! You sit there, stunned. A few moments later, the power comes back on. You will have to go through the tedious process all over again.*

You:
1.) Scream out loud and curse the power company gods for their cruelty. For good measure, you sneer and shake a fist at your computer, too. You then go and pour yourself a stiff drink.

2.) Force a laugh at the timing and figure it's either a sign from the heavens that you're not supposed to buy that item, or things will be easier the second time around.

Debrief: After having read so much of this book, forgive us, but if you were even drawn to the first response, you are so busted! Go back a few chapters and try a quick review. Remember the idea about how little control you have in life?

Or those discussions about the awful inevitables and the idea of *anticipating* the glitch, stitch, or hitch? Do the words Control Release Form ring a bell? Oops, it appears that the lecture gods came down from their mountaintop and took over for a moment. Sorry!

If, by any chance, you chose the second option, advance to "Go" and collect your $200.00. Simply put, you can shrug off life's minor inconveniences with a smile—or feed your stress demons with a scowl. If you have to do something over again, you may as well do it without the self-inflicted pain.

It was Shakespeare who said, "Sweet are the uses of adversity." What good are your blessing skills unless you meet up with situations where you can actually put them into practice?

Practice Makes Perfect

There's an old, old song titled *You Always Hurt the One You Love*, but in most cases, the one you actually hurt is yourself. Consider, for example, how many people complain and grouse about a situation long after it's over. An irritating incident that lasted maybe half a minute by the clock is kept alive and vivid for days—or maybe weeks—through the re-telling or reliving.

With every iteration, the situation worsens and the storyteller—the "victim"—gets more aggravated. What's up with that? Let other people shoot themselves in the foot if they so desire, but why would you want to sign up for hardship duty? Here are some suggestions for keeping the awful inevitables in perspective:

1.) Knowing that comedy is actually tragedy tempered by the passing of time, remind yourself what a good story this will make one day. Who knows, you might end up a serious contender in the "who can top this" category the next time you compare such moments with your friends.

2.) When you do something dumb, don't waste time beating yourself up or calling yourself stupid. Lighten up and let it go. Pretend you're starring in a sitcom, and you just gave an Emmy award-winning performance.

3.) If anyone tries to help you out of a self-inflicted jam, don't focus on your embarrassing mistake and blow it out of proportion. Instead, take note of how nice people can be when the chips are down.

4.) If you've publicly embarrassed yourself, what the heck. We all mess up. Give the observers a moment of feeling superior. If they don't know you, no big deal. And if they do, just kick your wait lifting skills into gear. Eventually these witnesses will take their rightful turn and do something dumb, and then you'll be even.

5.) Teach yourself to be amused—rather than annoyed—when irksome things happen. Perfect this response and you will spend more time smiling. You'll feel more blessed than stressed.

Instant Blessings: Handling the Irks, Jerks, and Quirks With a Smirk

Stuff will happen. You already know this. Now take a moment to imagine what your life might be like if you combined a little creativity with your sense of humor so you could stress less and bless more.

Here's the question—will your getting snarky or short-tempered stop the rain, enlighten muddleheaded motorists, make elevators speed to your floor, cause lines to move faster, make your cell work better in a dead zone? Getting all hyper over these things only affects you. It doesn't do squat for inanimate objects or even other people! Bless these moments, don't obsess over them.

Stress is a big bully, and it will try to get away with as much as it can. Stress can get all fluffed up and look ten times its size, but you don't have to be intimidated by the special effects. You don't have to let it push you around.

Like letting the air out of a balloon, you can whip stress down to size S instead of XXL. How do you neutralize the bully? Ridicule it. Mock it. Laugh at it, and you'll put stress in its rightful place. Here are some examples:

O *Bless this bleeping bottom feeder for presenting me with an opportunity to perfect my patience...*
O *Bless this knot-headed ninny for giving me a shot at practicing my tolerance...*
O *Bless this muckered mess for providing me with an occasion to regain my perspective...*
O *Bless this shambles of a situation for supplying me with a chance to use my sense of humor...*

If You Bless, You'll Decompress

How could anyone possibly utter any of these sentences with a straight face? Create your own outlandish, smirky statements to use when stress reports for duty. Memorize them, and as the doctor says, take as needed. Release that playful inner imp of yours and have some fun. Enjoy your taste of emotional independence.

When you bless your stress creatively, cleverly, and continuously, you whittle down the dimensions of that bloated, blathering stress bully until there's nothing left to fear.

What might happen if people were to personally and playfully bless their stressful moments instead of agonizing over them? What would it be like if they blessed (instead of obsessed) when things didn't go the way they wanted?

What a different world it could be if people decided to flow instead of blow when "it" hits the fan, and hey, it's really not all that difficult. It only takes a turn of mind to avoid such self-imposed anxiety. Are you ready to make the shift?

Stressing the Blessing

Here, for your reading pleasure, is a bounty of blessings, a plethora of prayers, a mass of meditations, a gaggle of graces. Call it what you will, we have tried to be comprehensive in creating this collection and hope you will be touched by the intent and implications. We hope you will enjoy and appreciate these light-hearted blessings and invocations:

Faithful Christian:

Thank you, Jesus, for blessing me with the presence of this depraved soul who is getting on my last nerve. I'm comforted to know that my spirit will be enriched if I ask WWJD—but, dear Lord, did you ever just want to smite someone?

Optimistic New Ager:

Having been blessed with this annoying creature from the bottom of the food chain who is attempting to push my buttons, I affirm my ability to draw upon a higher power so I can rise to the occasion. Surely I can't have asked for this hardship, but the universe will favor me if I cope.

Gentle Jew:

Holy Moses, I thought there were only 12 plagues—this person makes number 13, and the locusts are looking better every minute. Dear God, you parted the Red Sea; please help me find a way to graciously part with this person!

Practicing Buddhist:

People do what they will. Things happen, time passes. Nothing is forever. With the one who stands before me now, that impermanence is a blessing. Soon we will both be on our way, only one of us having experienced enlightenment.

Devout Muslim:

Allah has blessed me by bringing this ignorant individual into my life. Knowing that the actions I take will ultimately influence my destiny, I shall bide my time and bite my tongue with only a little bit of blood letting, for such restraint promises unearthly rewards.

Enduring Universalist:

Having been blessed with the company of this person who is currently masquerading as a blithering blockhead, I must remember that it's not my place to judge. There is good in everyone, although some suppress their goodness far better than others.

Nondenominational Curmudgeon:

It's a blessing in disguise that such a nattering ninny has come into my life. If nothing else, I can be grateful that I am so much more perceptive and patient than the person I'm trying to tolerate at this moment.

Ardent Atheist:

There is no higher power to either blame or credit for this galling joker who is getting on my nerves. Knowing I will receive no supernatural reward for my suffering, I shall forget this no-win situation as soon as it's over and go have a good meal instead.

Ambivalent Agnostic:

While I cannot state with certainty that God does or does not exist, I do know it's my responsibility to exercise self-control when dealing with someone who is acting like a missing link.

A friend suggested we also include the any-denominational, coy comment so often cooed by Southern Belles, regardless of the mean spirited, dark, or sinister thoughts they may be secretly harboring: *Why, bless your heart!*

A Blessing a Day Keeps the Stressing Away

Even if none of these blessings are exactly right for you, we hope you've been inspired to create your own. Let the good twin—your inner imp— help you compose your personal quirky prayers or mantras so you can shrug off unnecessary stress in style.

Record your masterpieces in your Bless Your Stress journal so you can reread and memorize them. This way, you'll be ready, willing, and able the next time you run into the inevitable *Challenge O' the Day.* You'll find that facing your stress with a smirk is enjoyable, enlightening, and yes—even entertaining.

Blessings Beget Blessings

Why are we harping about these little everyday blessings? Because people sometimes too tightly hold onto the negatives in life. They don't realize that there's only so much mental space in your consciousness, and when you throw out the negatives, you make room for the positives. If you are hanging onto any old worries, anger, resentment, or regrets, toss them out, so you can add a little four-season sun room to the home within your heart.

Norman Cousins described life as an exercise in forgiveness. Forcing a smile helps you forgive, forget, and refocus on what really matters. Whenever you smile, you relax. In effect, you bless yourself. Such lightness disarms your defense mechanisms and opens up your mind and heart. Consider how many chances you'll have to bless all kinds of situations each and every day! We wish you a long and fruitful career of bestowing such blessings upon yourself and the world.

If you come up with an especially clever blessing, mantra, or prayer, contact us at www.BlessYourStress.com and we'll post it on the web site.

Living Well is the Best Revenge

Trekkies know and love the words, "Live long and prosper." Maybe you never thought of this well-worn phrase as a kind of blessing, but it rather sounds like one, doesn't it? Living long is a wonderful wish, yet a lot of people complain about getting old. How dumb (and ignorant) is that?

After all, another birthday means you still haven't checked into your reserved mini-suite at the Eternity Hotel. This is good news. Great news, actually. If you're getting older, it means you're still rife with life, alert and overt, and aimed toward the game. So show up, suit up, and stay up so you can hang out and play with the rest of us!

With age comes wisdom (well, at least that's the hope). In fact, it's one of the major benefits of packing on a few extra years. Things get easier. Perspective broadens. Attitudes mellow. Hot buttons get de-installed. Eyesight may get a little blurry, but foresight and vision sharpen. Things get more clear.

One small blessing behind the physical changes of aging is that you are still here to complain about your symptoms, and even compare them with your friends. It's always nice having someone to talk with about such things.

Hung on the Young

A quick look at our youth-obsessed culture explains why the aging process is viewed with downcast eyes. As a society we're pretty queasy about getting old. We don't honor our elders like some other cultures do. Looking youthful is the happenin' thing.

Fresh, new, youthful celebrities and sports figures constantly replace each other on the covers of magazines. Athletes and female actors over the age of thirty are considered geezers. Who can miss this not-so-subtle message? Young is good. Aging is b-a-d. Aging is something you want to avoid. Oh yeah?

Does this mindset suggest you're better off requesting an early check-out from Hotel Extant instead of extending your stay as long as possible? Who really cares how youthful you look if you can no longer put a fresh, moist haze on a mirror? Hey, cherish those wrinkles and signs of age!

Celebrate the fact that you're not stuck in a permanent horizontal plane or reduced to an urn full of dust on someone's mantle or closet shelf. If you woke up this morning, just think—you've still got another shot at it. Could that simple thought make aging more of a blessing rather than a curse?

Accepting the Age Stage

The good news is that old is "younger" than it used to

be. Today, people in their sixties are no longer stooped, pooped, or drooped. Instead, they're out whooping it up on the golf course and tennis court, or sweating at the gym.

Today's sixty-somethings are comparable to the forty-somethings of yesteryear. Look at it this way: signs of aging are signs of *life*. Why shy away from that? Granted, the law of gravity is having a heyday, but so what? Things could be worse than finding another gray hair or a new little crease on your face. Way worse!

While we consumers will age (should we be so lucky), some of our classic childhood icons maintain a perpetually youthful cachet. You'll never see ads for Cellulite Barbie or Double Chin Ken with adjustable love handles. Even GI Joe, as old as he is, doesn't come in a beer belly motif. Thin, young, and attractive is the ideal. Of course, now that cosmetic surgery has come of age, people can take measures to stay perpetually young looking, like the dolls and action figures of their youth.

There's a lot of potential humor in this subject—for example, it's downright laughable that the women advertising anti-aging creams are barely out of puberty! And if those miracle potions we put on our faces are so effective, how come our fingertips don't look younger?

Age Old Expressions

If you're under forty, start thinking about how you want to age. Take care of yourself now. As people sometimes say, it wasn't raining when Noah started working on the ark. He thought ahead, and with a little bit of help, you can, too. Besides the optimistic fact that you're still breathing, there are some great perks that come with age.

You gain a stronger sense of self. You are far less hung up and insecure. You care less about what other people think, and that's a real blessing. You develop your own style of dress. You speak your mind, tactfully (we hope) but openly. You're less inhibited.

Being older gives you a chance to really be yourself, and once in awhile, even do something outrageous in a classy way. The Red Hat Club is one example of flaunting one's years instead of falling prey to the social perils of senior status.

They say it's never too late to have a happy childhood, and it's never too late to find your soulmate, either. We know a couple who fell in love and married toward the top rung of middle age. As committed, loving partners, they have vowed to take each other in their arms and dance every time they hear their song, *Unchained Melody,* regardless of where they may be. When skeptics ask, "Even if you're somewhere like the mall or a grocery store?" they look at each other, smile, and say yes. Coming of age just doesn't get any better than that!

Are the Glasses Half Full, Half Empty, or What?

If you're over forty, you may be grabbing your reading glasses every time you pick up this book. Eyeglass commercials are hysterical because everyone in the ad (except the pets) is sporting a pair of specs. Stretching this metaphor to its extreme, let us be so bold as to ask: are the lenses through which you look at life as clear and correctly adjusted as they could be? Of course, we're talking perspective here, not prescription, but you get the point.

Whether people choose to wear rose-colored or shaded

glasses, they pretty much get out of life what they expect. As Thoreau said, "It is not what you look at, it's what you see." There are people who see life through the eyes of a winner, looking for, and appreciating all that's there. But those who only look for what isn't there end up whining about everything that's missing. Winners. Whiners. Which of these types feel more stressed? Or blessed?

This is how it goes—you can feel bad because you're not quite as strong, swift, or sharp as you once were. Or you can feel grateful about all the things you can still do—and do pretty darned well.

Homeward Bound

One of the challenges of staying in the game for extra innings is that you might find yourself in the position of caregiving or assisting your aging parents—or dealing with adult "kids." Or both at the same time. In our society, people are living longer, though many become ill or frail, requiring daily attention or specialized professional care.

Kids who once left home sometimes come back to the nest, with ruffled feathers (and egos), after college or their dream job fizzles out. But a nest once emptied, like a map refolded, is never quite the same. This is why baby birds, once fledged, never return to the nest. But sometimes our kids fly back for more than a visit, and as much as we love them, it can be a challenge trying to find the right fit.

A friend of ours, while having a "sandwich generation moment," wailed, "How much more of this can I take? My parents won't die and my kids won't grow up!" Watching over, caring for, worrying about, and, at some point, saying goodbye to aging parents is one of the mixed blessings that comes with outliving some of your peers.

Hero Sandwich

Coping with the mental, physical, and financial demands of the sandwich generation requires heroic effort and coordinated contributions from every family member. Alas, that doesn't always happen. One of our friends, whose siblings refused to help, took over sole caregiving responsibilities when their mother became gravely ill. While Ann didn't necessarily bless her self-absorbed sisters, she did have the presence of mind to let go of any ill will, knowing that holding onto anger or resentment would be self-defeating.

Our friend discovered that jumping off the fast track ended up being as much a gift for herself as her mother. For the first time in her life, Ann had the opportunity to simply be with her mom. She would read to her, feed her, or just sit and hold her hand.

Ann was able to give back some of the love her mother had bestowed on her from childhood through adulthood. When her mother died, our friend had the satisfaction of knowing she had done all she could, and as she says, you can't put a dollar figure on the bank in your heart.

If you're at the point where it's your turn to step up to the plate, Karen Twichell's book *The Caregiver's Journey* may help you cope. Support groups, good friends, outside help, a clear conscience, and the practice of taking one day at a time can help keep you from feeling as if your caregiving responsibilities will never end. If you're in this position, remember to take good care of yourself, too.

Last Wishes

It's easy to sense the sadness and regret embedded in the phrase "if only." How many people have lamented late in life, "If I'd known I was going to live this long, I would've taken better care of myself!" Maybe you can relate. Of course, it's impossible to slide through life with no regrets, but some chronic malcontents will make a point of winding down with a lengthy list of last-minute woes.

The acerbic Fran Lebowitz sums it up for these types: "There is no such thing as inner peace. There is only nervousness and death." Given that tone, you can imagine the final reflections of the worriers, whiners, and complainers of the world as they drift into the lobby and slowly saunter toward the registration desk of the Everlasting Inn. Here might be the deathbed wishes of:

The Worriers
If only I'd done a better job of expressing my fears and insecurities! If only I had done a better job of hand wringing and stewing I could have died happy.

The Whiners
Oh, ain't it awful! If only I had planned better for this moment, I could have had a longer list of things to whimper and wail about. Things just never work out for me!

The Complainers
If only I'd complained more and felt less grateful throughout my life, I could have died fully discontent. But I know that's not gonna happen.

You know what the winner list would look like: fondest memories, loved ones and friends, achievements, treasured places and times. Here's a thought: it wouldn't hurt to record your favorite recollections. The actor Gene Wilder calls it a "Memory Treasure Chest."

Do you have one? This would make a great entry in your Bless Your Stress journal. Your cherished memories would make a wonderful place to revisit on a rainy day or one of those moments when you feel a little down.

Here are a few suggestions for keeping yourself in the winners circle, so you can have more fun and less frustration in every aspect of your life. We hope you'll find a few of these ideas personally appealing and that you will start putting them into practice immediately:

Strategies for Low-Stress Living

1) At home, at work, or in consumer situations, don't tick off the person who has the power (or ability) to give you what you want or need from them.

2) At work, if you're having a bad day, try to keep it a secret. Whomever you come in contact with, whether customers or workers, probably just wants you to be reasonably civil, so give it a try. You never know—some of them may be having a worse day than you. Force a little smile, find some small thing to feel grateful about, and you might be able to trade in that lousy mood for a free upgrade.

3) If you've got a beef about something, go to the person who can resolve or rectify the matter instead of wasting time griping to the innocent, uninvolved, and indifferent.

4) If you feel fat, stuffing yourself will only feel good until you swallow. Expect a big serving of guilt for dessert. Make a deal with yourself that you will spend ten minutes exercising or journaling before you put anything in your mouth. This can help stave off bouts of food abuse.

5) If you're building up a mental hairball about an issue, spit it out. Indirect anger (tsks, sighs, dirty looks, rolled eyes, clamming up, being sarcastic) is ineffective on two counts. First, you're being emotionally dishonest about what's bugging you, and second, the other person can choose to ignore your unhappy hints.

6) If day after day, your body feels like you were "rode hard and put away wet," start taking better care of yourself. Don't let stiff, achy muscles or tension and anxiety become your normal state. Address your stressors. Smile and laugh more. Breathe more deeply. Walk, exercise, and stretch more to enhance your health and well-being, a little bit at a time.

7) If you are extremely unhappy in your job, find something that suits you better. If that's impossible, then take up a hobby or pastime that rejuvenates your spirit. Staying in a job you hate is like subdividing your soul and selling it off plot by plot. There's no eternal reward for self-inflicted suffering and life is too short for such sacrifice.

8) You are in charge of what goes on in your head and comes out of your mouth. The words you think and say affect your outlook, shape your perceptions, and influence your actions. Instead of trying to control the universe, take charge of your personal "youniverse." Monitor and control what you think, say, feel, do, and put in your body.

9) When stress strikes, don't act like a victim. Think "unsinkable" instead. Open your heart and mind, mobilize your inner resources, and rally your positive energy. Do what the champions

do: bring out your best, even in the worst of circumstances. Whiner, no. Winner, yes!

10) Take time to feed your spirit. Time is the precious commodity of the 21st century, and too many people suffer from time deprivation. Keep reminding yourself that you are no longer living in an era of time management; you are living in an era of choice management. Your time on this earth is limited; choose well.

A World of Blessings

In doing our research for this book, we found it fascinating that all the major religions, spiritual philosophies, and yes, even the secular viewpoints, have so much in common. Each has its own way of saying live lightly, let go, and seek out joy.

Bless Your Stress praises, endorses, blesses, and embraces all iterations of this simple, wise message in all languages, denominations, and derivations. Given the resounding redundancy in the themes, apparently this is a message every human being needs to be reminded of, again and again.

For example, Christians are encouraged to make a joyful noise unto the Lord, and Muslims are told that the gates of paradise will open for those who make others laugh. Judaism encourages not only the joys of the spirit, but those of the body and mind as well, and Buddhism teaches that all things are perfect exactly as they are. As for the humanists, they are committed to seeking as much purpose and fulfillment as they can in the here and now, figuring this is pretty much it.

People of faith and nonbelievers alike share a simple and delightful message that so strongly resonates within the heart, spirit, and mind: *Lighten up. Let go. Celebrate your existence.* It's no coincidence that you have heard this theme time and again from a multitude of sources. Maybe, during hard times, you've encouraged yourself or others with these universal thoughts.

Let go of the stress, find something to bless. Every chapter in this book, in its own way, is about lightening up, letting go, and living fully so you can not only explore the undiscovered terrain in your life, but enjoy the journey, too. Isn't that what happiness is all about?

Chapter 10
Profess Your Stress

RUBES ™

By Leigh Rubin

5-27

"Congratulations, Bob, you made it!
Just watch your step. ... As I'm sure you've
heard by now, all dogs go to heaven."

Chapter 10
Profess Your Stress

It is only possible to live happily ever after on a day to day basis.
—Margaret Bonnano

Moving On

We hope you now have a good grasp on what stress is, and how it can affect you if you don't take charge and set some limits. Maybe you've taken a long look at your life and scrutinized the places where stress has moved in, unpacked its bags, set up housekeeping, programmed the remote, and even left some of its dirty socks on the floor.

If you haven't already given this unwelcome tenant its walking papers, now is the time. When it comes to stress, occasional brief visits are acceptable, but no more long-term occupancy. It's time for stress to move out and you to move on!

Making Change

If you've faithfully read this book, reflected on the ideas, and actually put some of them into practice, give yourself a pat on the back. If you've done all that, and completed at least some of the exercises, you're well on your way toward letting go of old habits and establishing new ones. In this chapter, you'll continue broadening your perspective and taking on the big picture.

By now you have a stronger sense of what life is about (for you), and how you can make the world a better place, one step at a time. Like the childhood game of connect the dots, when you attach the everyday details of living with your mission and purpose, everything tends to fall into place. But before we get to that, you have one last quiz to take.

Let's Play Guess Your Stress!

Situation: *It's a beautiful day, and you have the afternoon off. You drive to your favorite nature area, park your car, and head out for a much-needed walk in the woods. The sun is shining, birds are singing, and squirrels are scurrying about. Life is good.*

Half an hour later, your mind and spirit satisfied, you slip into your car. Then you sniff. Hmmm, could some gangster dog have broken in and soiled your car while you were gone? You jump out and check. It's your left foot. Your new waffle-sole sport shoe is filled with a heap of dog poop. You find a twig, sit down, remove your shoe, and dig and gouge with your crude, inadequate tool. Shoe back on, you now do the shoe tread shuffle, scuffing and dragging your foot up one side and down the other in the deep grass. You return to the gravel parking lot for a last swipe.

You spot a drinking fountain. No way! Even if you wanted to be so crass, you can't lift your foot that high. After a little more dancing in the dirt, you rinse your hands in the fountain and decide to head home where you'll complete the cleanup. As you open the car door, a clueless looking dog owner and unleashed canine about the size of a water buffalo burst out of the woods.

You:
1.) Turn to the person and yell, "I don't see any plastic bag in your hand! Are you one of those rude dog owners who refuses to pick up after your animal? There oughta be a fine for people like you!"

2.) Quietly get into your car and drive away, thinking it could have been worse. You remember a woman once telling you that on the day of her marriage, in veil and full-length gown, she stepped in a doggie pile on her way from the car to the church.

Debrief: Heap happens. Sometimes those graceless

moments simply can't be avoided. Of course, you could buy smooth-soled shoes next time. That might help a little. But sometimes, like the song says, "You're just a bug on the windshield of life."

Other times, as in the scene above, you might be one of the wipers. If you have the resilience to rebound from messy situations like this and take the inconvenience in stride, you've mastered at least some of the principles that help you bless rather than stress. Congratulations!

Signs of Life

We all have our own mental scrapbook of moments and memories, significant experiences that help shape and mold our character. You are the sum of these experiences, good, bad, or neutral, and you have the capacity for rising above the less-than-wonderful ones.

You might recall the discussion in chapter five about childhood impressions and how early messages can either inhibit (or inspire) your confidence, and break down (or boost) your self-esteem. Whether these moments helped or hindered you is connected to the kind of temperament you were born with.

If you were a troublesome kid like one of your authors (hint: Leslie), you may find solace in this section. If you were more of a model child like your other author (hint: Mimi), feel free to skip over this part. However, if you are the parent of a contrary child you suspect might have been switched at birth, stay tuned. You see, the very traits and qualities that got you into trouble as a kid are the ones that have helped make you successful as an adult.

If you were a mouthy, sneaky, or rebellious child—or the family misfit, take heart. And if you have a child who fits that description, there is hope. Of course, in the case of your child, like West Coast election returns, expect a time delay. Buff up your heavy wait lifting skills; it'll be worth it.

Early Stressing Can Bring Later Blessings

Sometimes adults expect kids to behave as if they're short grown-ups. But children's personalities come in extremes, and it takes time to smooth out those jagged edges. Temperament, plus vivid experiences, errors in perception, and personality quirks contribute to a youngster's exaggerated behaviors. In time, those radical traits will moderate, but this doesn't happen overnight. It can be hard to visualize a positive, more polished side of such obnoxious behaviors, but have faith. They are there, waiting to blossom.

Here are the eventual blessings that so often replace those early years of stressing:

O *Kids who talk too much have the potential of becoming "people" people. We know a woman who was hired by a bank as their official greeter. Her smiling face and ability to banter with anyone about anything could loosen the purse strings of even the tightest penny pincher.*

O *Stubborn kids often evolve into persistent adults. Look for this the next time you read a profile of some successful person who just didn't know enough to quit. While we don't have the inside scoop about her childhood, track and field Olympian Gail Devers is a stunning example of persistence. After recovering from Graves' Disease (where a misdiagnosis nearly resulted in having her feet amputated), she couldn't even walk the entire track. Since her recovery, she has once again competed and won numerous medals.*

❍ Curious kids—the ones who ask too many questions about how things work—often carry their knack for breaking, fixing, and "mixing" things into adulthood. Think of Tom and Ray, the Car Talk brothers, who entertain and inform car owners on their NPR show. Or Bill Nye the Science Guy. And soprano-voiced Julia Child, the pioneer of cooking shows. Who would have thought these individuals would create careers built around their inquisitive personalities and knack for fiddling with things?

❍ Cry babies often make compassionate listeners once they grow up. Maybe Oprah was a bit of a wailer when she was a kid. Or Dr. Phil. Probably not Dr. Laura, though. But think of the best listeners in your life, personal or professional, and consider how their gift of empathy and concern for others might have made them the subject of teasing or putdowns when they were little.

❍ Rebellious children often mature into independent thinkers or outstanding performers in their field. Apolo Anton Ohno, the brilliant Olympic short-track speed skater, was no longer a trouble-prone teen once he discovered this extremely demanding sport. Sometimes all we need is a suitable outlet for our excess energy.

❍ Kids who don't fit in (geeks, nerds) can become ingenious adults. Think of Steve Jobs or Bill Gates, and the empires they created as a result of their brain power. The humorous writers Sarah Vowell and David Sedaris were considered oddballs and misfits when they were young, but today they are celebrity authors with a dedicated following.

❍ Kids who lie or make up their own versions of reality might simply be walking on the wild side of their imagination. The creative Carl Hiaasen, Susan Isaacs, and Stephen King may have been quite the "storytellers" when they were kids. The same goes for Dave Barry or Janet Evanovich.

See? Those troublesome traits of youth have a good side, after all. Too bad this isn't common knowledge—better PR about our "dark side" could save some of us from early grief and self-consciousness. But as wonderful as your best characteristics may be now that you're a responsible, wise, and wonderful adult, there still exists a potential down side.

Just ask anyone who lives or works with you, and they will verify that the same qualities for which you receive compliments are connected to the behaviors that garner the most criticism. You can run, but you can't hide. We hate to be the bearers of bad tidings, but face it—sometimes you drive people up the wall.

Play the Deck You're Dealt

It's always helpful to think of a weakness as an overextension of a strength. For example, persistence is an admirable quality, but relentlessness is not. Friendly and outgoing is great, but babbling is not. You get it. The secret is balance, smoothing out those old, rough edges before you trip over them.

First of all, it might help to think of your best qualities as your "trump cards." They're your strong suit—your saving grace, your personal advantage—but this delicate combination needs to played in the right amount at the right time. This is what it means to bring out your best under the worst of circumstances.

Treatment for the Toxic Types

But don't get too excited yet—unfortunately, people may not always perceive your trump card as your best play. They may be jealous, unable to comprehend, or too self-absorbed to fully understand your actions. They may resist, criticize, or withdraw. Not exactly the stuff of your dreams! And while you want to be tuned in to others and compassionate to their needs, you don't want to be intimidated by other people's negative or controlling attitudes.

Eleanor Roosevelt reminds us that no one can make you feel inferior without your consent. With a blend of tact and reserve you can stand your ground and maintain your integrity. You can profess your positive self-regard by avoiding chronically toxic people—the ones who are good at trying to make you feel bad about yourself.

If, in your job, you must tolerate toxic coworkers (people who are chronically cranky, negative, or critical), don't panic. Push the Pause button instead. Ask yourself the "three calming questions" from chapter three. Create a protective mental bubble for yourself every time someone spouts off. Slather yourself with W.A.R.T. Begone.

You know that worry, anger or resentment will only hurt you and won't do jack to the other party. Here's the best part: when these uppity individuals discover they're no longer getting to you, they'll probably clam up. What fun can they possibly get out of pushing buttons that you have permanently disconnected?

For the Holidaze or Other Homely Visits

If you look forward to holiday festivities and family gatherings, skip over this paragraph. But if your clan tends to whip up a big batch of high-toxic stew every time it gets together, you can "immunize" yourself from their noxious nattering. The following suggestions may help you arrive and leave with impunity:

1.) Arrive late and leave early to limit your exposure as much as possible.

2.) If a conversation gets dicey, practice common sense and don't throw in your two cents.

3.) Take frequent bathroom breaks whether you need them or not.

4.) Before you make a statement, pause and take a nice deep breath to prevent foot-in-mouth disease.

5.) Keep your face neutral. Avoid sighing, eye rolling, or tsking, no matter how tempting it is.

6.) Remember the Control Release Form you signed earlier in the book. Even if you've tried to be the family peacemaker in the past, how well has it worked? Ask yourself if it's a good idea to referee in a losing game.

7.) Carry your Gratitude List card and haul it out for a quick read when you need a positive reminder.

8.) Instead of feeling critical or resentful, accept that these people are who they are. Bless the fact that you no longer have to interact with them on a daily basis.

9.) Give up wishing that members of your family would magically transform. If they've been this way for years, they probably aren't going to change. Save yourself the energy and stress.

10.) After you leave, give yourself a big blessing for the life you've chosen to create for yourself.

Hold 'Em or Scold 'Em?

It takes time to learn that you don't have to be taken down by someone else's spite, meanness, or moodiness. Although it takes some work, you can teach yourself to remain emotionally independent of other people's judgment or chronic negativity. Here's a fairly common example— let's say you tend to be upbeat, but your spouse or partner is more on the glum side. You're in a good mood, you walk in the door, and there's a chill in the air. It feels as if you've just been transported into the Temple of Doom.

Your first reaction might be, "What have I done?" Perhaps nothing. Your second reaction might be, "How can I fix this situation?" But you signed the Control Release Form, remember? Alas, you're not in charge of someone else's moods. You're no longer captain of the Cosmic Rescue Squad; you're just you.

Of course, you can ask how you might be able to help, and if you get no response, quietly go about your business without getting uppity or putting on your own shroud of woe. After all, one of you has to stay functional! Be open to discussion, be kind, patient, and accepting. Sometimes the best thing you can do is nothing.

We learned this strategy from a good friend who practiced this kind of restraint for years. Eventually her husband was able to master his moods without her intervention. Today he's a pretty happy guy, and their relationship has spanned three decades.

An Act of Mastery

Actor Michael Caine summed up the love he feels for his craft in one sentence: "Rehearsal is the work; performance is the pleasure." Those words apply not only to acting, but to life. Perhaps Caine's comment inspires you to consider what *you're* rehearsing day after day. Stressing or blessing? Unthinkable or unsinkable self-talk?

Do you shrink when the stress bully reports for duty, or bless life's bloopers with a smile? Think about how well you have acted so far in this limited run performance called life, and if there is room for improvement.

Mastery is the result of building on your strengths, and you have many. Take a moment to think about something you're good at—really good. Don't be modest. Identify a skill, talent, or special knack your friends or family praise and admire. Let's say you dance or sing well, you're good with words, or you're a computer whiz. Perhaps you've perfected a parlor trick, such as tying a knot in a maraschino cherry stem using only your teeth and tongue.

The point is, there are moments when people marvel at your mastery. Now, think of the ways you can practice your *mental* mastery (as covered in chapters four though six), and apply these skills to aspects of your life that really count.

You may not win an Academy Award, but when you profess your stress, you transfer your thoughts and beliefs into action. When you take the bad along with the good, you shower yourself with the kinds of little rewards that add up to big satisfaction for what you've achieved.

Mind Your Mastery

You probably knew we wouldn't let this big issue go by without inviting you to make a few comments in your Bless Your Stress journal:

O   It's important to recognize your best qualities so you can master your ability to play your trump card at the right time. Identify your two major strengths: childhood traits that may have been awkward or troublesome when you were little, but helped you become who you are today.

O   Now, describe how you might overuse or misapply these natural assets (this is where the criticism from others comes from).

O   Describe how you could adjust or modify the not so wonderful side of your two major strengths so you can minimize their less desirable aspects.

Mind Your Mastery at Work, Too

The workplace is quite an amazing study, when you stop and think about it. A bunch of people, thrust together by chance, not by choice, are expected to get along and go along, regardless of their differences. What a concept! Not only must you contend with people and their personalities, your *workplace* has its own unique characteristics, too.

Some work cultures are task-focused, productive, and centered around competence rather than specific credentials. Other cultures are more bureaucratic in nature, focusing on roles and formal positions instead of personal capabilities. Some are a blend of both, like a combo meal.

It's not just the work climate you have to contend with, but the individuals within that culture, too. Some bosses just want you to do your job, while others expect you to fulfill your role. No one gives you a cheat sheet to figure this stuff out. It's your job to assess the system in which you work, and to profile the major players who are calling the shots. It ain't called work for nothing!

What is the Sound of One Hand Slapping?

Maybe you've gotten into trouble because you didn't jump through the proper hoops to complete a delegated task. This wasn't a case of *not* doing your job. In your manager's eyes, it was a case of not doing your job *right*. Or perhaps you were criticized for "procrastinating" when you were actually *waiting* for instructions.

In the second situation, your supervisor was expecting you to "just do it" while you were trying to figure out exactly how it was supposed to be done. Sometimes these culture clashes and style conflicts are enough to make you want to curl up in the corner of your cubicle and hibernate for the winter!

It pays to understand your work climate, and the operating values of your manager or supervisor. Don't shirk your work—you have to do your job while trying to mesh with the environment, personalities, and preferences of those around you.

This isn't always easy. You may not be blessed with the best job in the world, nor the best boss. But it's always a good idea to do a good job anyway. Always think "references." There may be a day far off in the future that you decide to bail, and if you've been a consistently good performer, you'll have nothing to worry about. As we say in an earlier chapter, success is the best revenge.

Help! I've Fallen Down on the Job and Can't Get Back Up

For all the bad managers or companies in the world, here's a comforting thought—people usually find ways to circumvent faulty systems or poor leadership. For example, there are restaurants that have a policy of giving only one check per table, and the managers usually like to blame it on their computer system.

But if you treat your servers well, most of them will split the check anyway. That old saying about motivation—people will find a way to do what they want to do—certainly works in this instance. Hey, if a server wants a nice tip, what better way to get one than to bend the rules and make a customer feel special? It's almost as fun as having a secret handshake.

Employees also have clever ways of expressing their negative feelings toward an oppressive, inconsistent, or unkind culture. Gallows humor—often intelligent and painfully on target—can help liberate unhappy workers from an onerous, regimented work environment. You can get a sense of an organization's culture by noting what people jokingly say about their employer and their work atmosphere, but also take a good look at what they hang on their office walls. You can learn a lot about the employer—and the employee.

If you're reading this at work, are you thinking it's time to take a little stroll so you can do a quick scan and see what's out there? Or are you about to do an extreme makeover of your office, just in case?

By its very nature, work can be frustrating or fulfilling, and a lot of that depends on you. It's tempting to think that the other party is the problem, and in some instances this may be true, but so what? Knowing what's wrong isn't enough because you can't control other people's behavior, only your own. This is a truism that every disgruntled employee has to understand and accept. Guess it's time to bless that work stress, along with every other kind in your life!

A Peace of Work

One of our seminar participants was on the brink of having to take a stress leave. She and her boss had a horrendous relationship and she was suffering from mental distress, stomach problems, physical pain, and sleeplessness. This woman was desperate for relief, but couldn't retire, nor did she want to lose her seniority. Her boss refused to give her a transfer, so she was stuck. After attending some seminars and reading a few books she decided to work with a therapist.

Some months later, by chance, we ran into her. After our hesitant, "How's work?" she smiled and said, "Great!" Knowing how grim her situation had been, we were burning with curiosity. "Did your boss die? Retire? Quit? Transfer? Get promoted?" She said no. We then asked, "Did you retire? Quit? Transfer? Get promoted?" She shook her head.

"So," we asked, "What was it that changed?" Her answer was, "Me!" She had realized that if something didn't change soon, her health would be at risk. And it was clear that her boss wasn't going to budge. This woman finally grasped that she could either continue making herself sick over these circumstances, or she could make herself well, in spite of them.

In essence, she created her own Control Release Form. In a few months, her physical symptoms disappeared and peace of mind returned. Simply put, spending so much time stressing had left no room in her life for blessing. Her story is one we will always remember, and we hope you will, too.

Make Work Work For You

We hope your situation will never be that extreme. We hope you work in an environment that is enjoyable and filled with opportunities to learn and build new skills. But just in case, here are a few suggestions that might make work feel a little less like work. Some of these points will also apply to your personal life, as well.

Eight Ways to Make Work Less Work

1.) Play Team. *You don't have to love the people you work with. You just have to get along with them so you can be a contributing member of the team. Keep your finger near the Pause button, and don't get carried away with judgment or criticism. This way, you can leave work feeling good about yourself instead of bad about others.*

2.) Cooperate. *Work might be described as a mutual exchange of information and services. Why be an obstructionist? Make it easy for people to do their jobs; give them what they want or need from you. Who knows, they might just do the same for you. Even if they don't, if your boss is watching it will make you look very good!*

3.) Stay upbeat. *Keep your attitude in the right place. There's more to life and work than hanging around and waiting for your boss to die. Do a good job anyway. You might get a better offer from somewhere else, and getting a good recommendation from the person you report to never hurts.*

4.) Learn from others. *Use difficult people as a project for your self-improvement, not theirs—unless transforming others is part of your job description. Remember, trying to teach someone else what you think they need to know is about as easy as herding cats.*

5.) Tolerate differences. *Accept other people's work styles, and maybe they'll be less critical of yours. Keep worry, anger, and resentment at bay so your tension level stays low. Keep the W.A.R.T. Begone handy, and heap it on whenever you need to.*

6.) Make work enjoyable. *The team that plays together stays together. In one of our client service centers, each employee had a white "I surrender" flag she waved from her cubicle when the pressure built up, offering everyone much-needed comic relief. We think every office should have a rotating "Fun Captain" to keep the atmosphere light and low-stress.*

7.) Avoid communication overload. *Instead of sending an e-mail every time you have a thought, make a note. When you've amassed a few items, do something radical; take a short stroll across the office and talk with the person face to face. Discuss communication preferences so you know which approach works best (e-mail or in person) with different individuals.*

8.) Stay at your peak. *Take good care of yourself at work. Stay away from junk food and go light on the caffeine. Drink more water. Make your work space as ergonomically correct as possible to avoid needless aches and pains. If your job requires a lot of sitting, get up every now and then. Stand up, stretch, or take a quick walk so you don't end up feeling like Frankenstein or The Mummy every time you get out of your chair.*

Work Teams That Laugh, Last

No matter how serious your work may be, find ways to keep your workplace as enjoyable as possible. Think of the pressures mental health workers, special ed teachers, healthcare professionals, day care specialists, victim rights advocates, social workers, police officers, firefighters, and all of their assistants experience every day.

They and people in other intense, high-stress professions know the value of keeping things light whenever possible. They laugh, not at their clients, patients, students, or customers, but at themselves. Their humor is a healing tonic that allows them to remain effective in their highly demanding jobs. If they didn't laugh, they wouldn't last.

What If

Pressure-filled jobs or not, we all have our unique way of looking at the world. Here's a chance for you to evaluate your point of view. In your Bless Your Stress journal, or just in your head, please complete the following sentences:

I could do a better job if...

I would enjoy my work more if...

My relationships at home would improve if...

I know I'd feel better mentally and physically if...

There are essentially two ways to finish these statements and we invite you to carefully consider your responses to each item. You see, some people immediately add an "I" to the above statements. Here are two examples:

*I could do a better job if...**I were better at setting priorities.***

*I would enjoy my work more if...**I had a more positive outlook.***

These individuals emphasize precisely what *they* could do to personally alter or improve the situation. A psychologist would say they have an *internal* locus of control; in other words, they recognize that while you can't control what others do, you ultimately control what you do.

But there's another way to respond to the above items. Some people place their focus on outside circumstances. Here's how they would complete these statements:

*I could do a better job if...**my boss were to die / quit / retire / transfer / get promoted.***

*I would enjoy my work more if...**there weren't so many idiots around here.***

These individuals have an external locus of control; that is, they are affected by forces *outside* of themselves. They want the circumstances to change without their having to do anything. Rather than altering the situation, they continue to hope and wait for a miracle. Good luck with that! They fail to recognize that things won't change until they do. Think of the stress connected to this point of view.

You Be The Judge

Internal control or external emphasis: some people get it and some don't. In time, experience can teach you to recognize a mistake when you make one. But for the slow learners of the world, it may take a repeat performance (or a few) before the lesson sinks in. Alas, for some poor, distressed souls, life is an endless series of the same mistakes and crises. As the saying goes, "Good judgment is the result of experience. Experience is the result of poor judgment."

Life offers unlimited opportunities to learn, unlearn, and relearn, but not everyone values the process. Consider the hours some people spend learning how to operate their smart high-tech toys, but they wouldn't consider investing the same amount of effort in their own self-exploration. They might say, "Hey, I don't have time to read self-help books!"

or "Too much of that touchy-feely stuff gives me a headache." These individuals will spend days absorbing every word in a manual explaining how their new cell phone or PDA functions, but they have no curiosity whatsoever about how *they* function as human beings.

Deja` You

On the other hand, you've made the smart choice of doing your inner work. Just as you periodically upgrade hardware or software, you can consider yourself upgrade ready—and with a simple install, you can replace your old stressing software with the new blessing version. Here you are, the new, improved, upgraded, multifunction model with Control Panel features not available until now. You now possess new capabilities, and you can fully utilize your powerful new features as you choose.

As for operating manuals, reread *Bless Your Stress* several months from now. The words won't change, but you will! In fact, reread this, or any of your favorite self-help books from the past, and you'll stumble across a surprising number of good ideas you missed the first time around because you just weren't ready for them yet.

The Point of No Return

We've all been told that ignorance is bliss, but on his album *Natural Selection,* songwriter Mark Graham laments, "Life is hard, but life is hardest when you're dumb." Graham knows, and so do you, that life doesn't have to be so hard. It's a matter of outlook, choice, and consistency. You're the one who ultimately decides whether to launch your day with a "Good morning, God" or a "Good God, it's morning!" After reading this book you can't go back to old habits, and why would you want to?

Professing your stress puts you on the brink of opening yourself up to all your experiences, not just the easy ones. You'll handle uncertainty and adversity with more confidence. You'll get beyond the inconvenience of the moment because you will have the big picture in your head.

You won't get bogged down in life's little annoyances and awful inevitables because you will recognize the rewards of shrugging off the small stuff. The big stuff—that list of the five most important things in your life you feel so grateful for—is what really counts.

The Adventure Continues

Helen Keller, who was blessed with more stress than just about anyone you could think of, stands as an example of what can be achieved in the face of adversity. She said, "Security is mostly a superstition. It does not exist in nature nor do the children of humankind actually experience it. In the long run, life is either a daring adventure or nothing." Let the words of this amazing woman live in your heart every day. Let her remind you of what a precious gift you've been given. Let her words inspire you to seek "adventure" in times of challenge, uncertainty, and confrontation.

You possess unlimited potential. This means you don't just handle what life gives you, but you choose to learn from your experiences. As a result, you prevail over adversity and gain confidence in your judgment. You end up inspiring others, simply by your example. When you are bold and outrageous enough to make your life a daring adventure, you bless yourself with every good decision.

Live creatively—design your personal life blueprint, and decorate the edges with imagination and flair. Some people only use their creativity to falsify tax returns, or make up elaborate excuses. So much for ingenuity.

Too Blessed To Be Stressed?

Bless you for taking this message to heart and for spreading the good word about what you've learned here. Your changes and good deeds will be evident. The world is made better by one caring person at a time, and we could certainly use a legion of compassionate people. We've tried to do our part by writing this book and talking about these ideas to our audiences. We know you'll do your part, too.

As you read these last paragraphs, take a moment and tap into your inner dreamer—the creative, idealistic part of you that visualizes a better world, better relationships, a better you. Now imagine what your everyday life might be like if you let your inner idealist rearrange the furniture to make room for more blessings in your life.

Imagine That!

Imagine yourself taking a nice deep breath, smiling, and saying, "Yup, there it is..." when traffic clots up or that way-too-conscientious driver in front of you has the *audacity* to actually drive the speed limit. Imagine yourself bestowing a silent, smirky blessing on someone who is masquerading as a blockhead, and they're not even wearing their Jerk Alert ID Bracelet. Imagine yourself looking up to the heavens and enjoying a private laugh when you catch yourself commanding your computer to hurry up, or your microwave to get a move on.

Now imagine what the world might be like if everyone had the presence of mind to bless instead of stress—at least part of the time. Think about how much smoother life would be if you were surrounded by a multitude of smiles instead of scowls, grins instead of grimaces, and laughs instead of verbal lashes. It gives you something to shoot for, doesn't it?

All's Well that Ends Well

If you were forced to find one word that sums up this book, maybe you'd say "perspective." It's a rare quality these days. It's hard maintaining perspective in a noisy, distracting world that's busy knocking out 24/7 media reports filled with celebrity gossip, news that isn't really news, and exposure to hundreds of captivating commercials a day.

It's difficult keeping your perspective when social pressures are urging you to move faster, work harder, spend more than you can afford, and constantly upgrade what you've got so you can have it all, do it all, and be it all. For many people, this is the American Dream, but too often it turns into a nightmarish cycle of wanting and getting, getting and wanting that has no end. You can do better than this, and you know it.

Give yourself the gift of ongoing reflection. Take time to read, time to think, time to expand your horizons. Give yourself time to explore, time to ask essential questions about life and living such as:

Am I happy?

Is this what I really want to be doing with my life?

Am I truly living in line with my priorities?

What is my mission in life—what is my purpose?

And how is it that those idiotic, screaming, TV car salesmen actually attract any customers?

On Purpose

Robert Byrne said that the purpose of life is a life of purpose. If so much of life's purpose really is about lightening up, letting go, and celebrating your existence, there's no better time than now to make it happen. Embrace your purpose, live it to the best of your ability, and create your own happy ending. You'll not only be a positive influence on everyone you come in contact with, but you can also become your own unlimited source of inspiration.

We hope that, as a result of reading this book, you more clearly recognize the power of your potential as well as the power of your perceptions. The late Senator Paul Wellstone said, "Let there be no distance between the words you say and the life you live." Perhaps these wise, powerful words will charge your spirit and rally your reserve to do just that.

Join us in taking a last long moment to visualize the important role you can play, in both word and deed, to help your world become a less edgy, less fractious, more gentle, and more genteel place. Be assured that we are doing our part as well. Just imagine the bounty of blessings that could await us all, if we as a species could overcome our differences long enough to join forces in this noble effort!

By making the commitment to assess, confess, address, less, yes, finesse, press, bless, and profess life's stress, even one person can make a difference. You can make a difference. Day by day, you can actively contribute toward making the world a better place, especially for yourself and those you love. What higher purpose could there be than that?

A Final Note

In the spirit of full disclosure, we thought you would appreciate knowing that all of the Guess Your Stress quizzes are real, based on our experiences and those of our friends.

Look around, and you'll be able to play your own Guess Your Stress quizzes every day. We promise.

From Mimi: How I Bless My Stress

My twelve-year old nephew, Marky and I spent a delightful Saturday afternoon watching *Miracle,* a film documenting the U.S. Hockey team's 1980 Olympic win. For dinner, I planned to show Marky the oldest restaurant in Hollywood: the famous Musso & Frank Grill, where he could order from their oversized menu.

Our plans were foiled when I made a wrong turn. Stuck in traffic, I cursed myself and the entire LA freeway system. As Marky fell asleep, I called other restaurants, but it was Valentine's Day. No tables anywhere! Desperate, I headed for an Indian restaurant near my house, hoping for an Auntie Mame-like adventure. As we walked inside, Marky said "Eew. What's that smell?" He didn't like any of the food and was trying to escape into sleep. But then it happened.

At a nearby table, a familiar looking man caught my attention. It was Phil Jackson, the coach of Marky's favorite team, the Lakers. Knowing Marky collects autographs, I whispered, "Don't look now, but guess who's sitting behind you—Phil Jackson!"

This was perfect: Marky was wearing his basketball sweatshirt. We planned our strategy. As Phil finished dinner, Marky made his move. "Hi! My name is Mark Riley. I'm the center on my travel basketball team in Connecticut." Phil laughed, "You're too short to be a center." Marky continued, undaunted. "Well, sometimes I'm the power forward. Right now I'm visiting my aunt and we're coming to your game on Tuesday night." I could see Phil was enjoying this.

Marky continued. "You're my favorite coach of my favorite team and I was wondering if you would sign this for me?" Phil signed away with a smile, telling Marky to enjoy Tuesday's game. Marky said, "Good luck the rest of your season." He returned to the table, holding the precious paper. Phil had written, *To Mark, the center/ power forward. Best wishes, Phil Jackson.*

How much stress I could have avoided by trusting that things would turn out. I recognize there isn't much in life I can actually control. All I can do is watch a plan go awry and train myself to ask, "I wonder what the blessing will be." Because of my "wrong" turn I gave my nephew the most memorable night of his life, and a lesson worth remembering for myself.

From Leslie: How I Bless My Stress

In writing this book, I realized I've been blessing my stress for quite awhile. There was a time when, if I were washing dishes, reorganizing my office, or cleaning the bathroom, I'd feel "put upon" over having to do these chores. But now, I count my blessings that I'm healthy enough to do these bothersome tasks. It's a matter of perspective.

Likewise, I try to reframe the negatives. Instead of obsessing over what I don't have (beautiful hands and long, strong fingernails, for example), I'd rather think about the nifty things these hands of mine have done through the years—caring for my kids and grandkids, cooking, practicing calligraphy, making bracelets, and writing poetry, for example.

The year I began writing *Why Is Everyone So Cranky?*, I initiated a self-improvement practice—that of choosing one behavior a year to integrate into my daily routine. I learned that when you give yourself an entire year to work on a behavior, for once, time is on your side. The experiment worked so well, I included this idea in the book.

Two years later, I worked on becoming amused rather than annoyed over life's little irritations. This one practice has lightened my life by replacing everyday annoyances and frustrations with amusement, laughter, or levity. Now, when I screw up, stumble or fall, get lost, or have a situation spin out of control, my spontaneous response is to laugh (at myself, of course) rather than get upset. I have a sneaking suspicion that this is where the seeds of *Bless Your Stress* were sown.

If you're intrigued about the 365-day personal project, or adopting an annual theme, you can read more about them by simply visiting www.WhyIsEveryoneSoCranky.com.

About the Cartoons

You could call **Leigh Rubin** a sit-down comedian: in his own way, he delights in making other people laugh. Rubin took his first steps on the path to cartoon success in 1979, establishing Rubes Publications, his own publishing company, and distributing his own greeting cards. He began publishing the popular Notable Quotes in 1981.

Rubes, in the form that cartoon aficionados now know it, began appearing in newspapers in 1984 and the first paperback collection of Rubes was published in late 1988 by G.P. Putnam & Sons. Rubin's most recent series of books include *The Wild Life of...Love, Cats, Dogs, Pets, Cows and Farm Animals.*

Originally self-syndicated, Rubes is now distributed by Creators Syndicate to more than 400 newspapers worldwide. As one of the most popular single-panel cartoons, Rubes is a regular feature in SkyWest's United Express and Delta Connections, and Atlantic Southeast magazine. Rubes appears in major daily metropolitan papers such as the San Diego Union Tribune, the Rochester Democrat and Chronicle, the Winnipeg Free Press, the Washington Times, the Sacramento Bee, the Houston Chronicle, the Orange County Register, and the Los Angeles Daily News.

To see Leigh's books and a daily cartoon:
http://www.comics.com/creators/rubes/html/comic_books.html

Leigh's Publisher:
www.willowcreekpress.com/rubes

From Mimi: *There I was, flipping through the SkyWest Airline magazine when I saw this brilliant cartoon that summed up blessing your stress better than anything I had seen. I knew I had to track down that brilliant cartoonist, and I did. Leigh Rubin has turned out at least a cartoon a day for 19 years, and we feel blessed for his contributions to this book.*

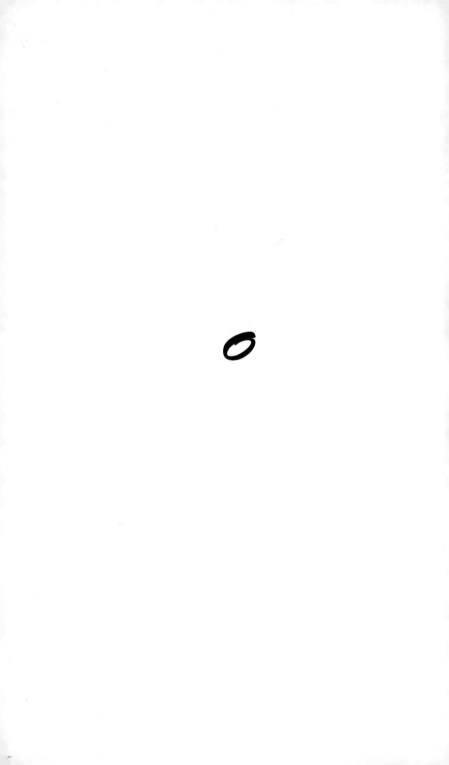